Brokering the Good Friday Agreement

Brokering the
Good Friday Agreement

The untold story

edited by MARY E. DALY

Brokering the Good Friday Agreement: the untold story

First published 2019
Royal Irish Academy, 19 Dawson Street, Dublin 2
www.ria.ie

ISBN 978-1-911479-09-3 (PB)
ISBN 978-1-911479-10-9 (pdf)
ISBN 978-1-911479-11-6 (epub)
ISBN 978-1-911479-12-3 (mobi)

British Library Cataloguing in Publication Data. A CIP catalogue record
for this book is available from the British Library.

Project Manager: Helena King
Editor: Brendan O'Brien
Design: Fidelma Slattery
Index: Eileen O'Neill

Printed in the UK by CPI Group

Royal Irish Academy is a member of Publishing Ireland,
the Irish book publishers' association

5 4 3 2 1

This publication has received support from

**An Roinn Gnóthaí
Eachtracha agus Trádála**
Department of
Foreign Affairs and Trade

CONTENTS

GLOSSARY OF NAMES

Gerry Adams, member of Provisional Sinn Féin, Sinn Féin president 1983–2018

Bertie Ahern, leader of Fianna Fáil 1994–2008, taoiseach 1998–2008

Dermot Ahern, Fianna Fáil politician, minister for foreign affairs 2004–8

Martti Ahtisaari, president of Finland 1994–2000, member of the Independent International Commission on Decommissioning in Northern Ireland, Nobel Peace Prize winner 2008

Julian Amery (1919–96), Conservative MP 1952–92, member of the Monday Club

David Andrews, Fianna Fáil TD 1977–2002, minister of state at Department of Foreign Affairs 1977–79, minister for foreign affairs 1997–2000

Robert Armstrong, principal private secretary to British prime minister 1970–9; permanent secretary, Home Office 1977–79; Cabinet secretary 1979–87

Donal Barrington (1928–2018), barrister, supreme court justice, author of Tuairim pamphlet *Uniting Ireland* 1957

Peter Barry (1928–2016), deputy leader of Fine Gael 1977–87, 1991–3; minister for foreign affairs 1982–7

Ray Bassett, Department of Foreign Affairs

Roy Beggs, Ulster Unionist Party, Westminster MP 1983–2005

Sandy Berger (1945–2015), United States national security advisor 1997–2001

Bill Benyon (1930–2014), Conservative MP 1970–92

Sir John Biggs-Davison (1918–88), Conservative MP 1970–88, member of Monday Club

Tony Blair, British prime minister 1997–2007

Sir Kenneth Bloomfield, permanent secretary to Northern Ireland power-sharing executive 1974, head of Northern Ireland civil service 1984–91

Leon Brittan (1939–2015), Conservative MP, home secretary 1983–5, EU commissioner 1989–99

Peter Brooke, Conservative MP 1977–2001, secretary of state for Northern Ireland 1989–92

Joe Brosnan, secretary-general, Department of Justice 1991–3; member of Independent Monitoring Commission

John Bruton, leader of Fine Gael 1990–2001, taoiseach 1994–7

Sir Antony Buck (1928–2003), Conservative MP 1961–93

Nicholas Budgen (1937–98), Conservative MP 1974–97

Robin Butler, principal private secretary to the prime minister 1982–85, Cabinet secretary 1988–98

David Byrne, attorney general 1997–9, EU commissioner 1999–2004

James (Jim) Callaghan (1912–2005), British home secretary 1967–70, foreign secretary 1974–7, prime minister 1977–9

Hugh Carey (1919–2011), governor of New York State 1975–82, one of the so-called Four Horsemen of US politics

Jimmy Carter, US president 1977–81

Peter Carrington (1919–2018), secretary of state for defence 1970–4, foreign secretary 1979–82

John Chilcot, civil servant, Home Office and Cabinet Office; permanent under-secretary of state for Northern Ireland 1990–7

Bill Clarke, US assistant secretary of state for political–military affairs 1989–92

Bill Clinton, US president 1993–2001

Gerard Collins, Fianna Fáil TD 1967–97, minister for justice 1977–81, 1987–9; minister for foreign affairs 1982, 1989–92

Padraic Collins, Department of Foreign Affairs

Tom Conaty, chair of Belfast Central Citizens Defence Committee and community activist, 1970s

Don Concannon (1930–2003), British Labour MP 1966–87, under-secretary of state for Northern Ireland 1974–6, minister of state for Northern Ireland 1976–9

Robin Cook (1946–2005), British Labour MP 1966–2005, foreign secretary 1997–2001

David Cooney, Department of Foreign Affairs

Brendan Corish (1918–90), leader of Irish Labour Party 1960–77, tánaiste 1973–77

Liam Cosgrave (1920–2017), leader of Fine Gael 1965–77, taoiseach 1973–7

Declan Costello (1926–2011), attorney general 1973–7

David Crouch (1919–98), Conservative MP 1966–87

Bernard Cullen, Department of Foreign Affairs

Austin Currie, member of Northern Ireland parliament 1964–72, member of Northern Ireland Civil Rights Association, founding member SDLP, Fine Gael TD 1989–2002, minister of state at Department of Justice 1994–7

John Cushnahan, leader of the Alliance Party 1984–7

Cardinal Cahal Daly (1917–2009), Roman Catholic bishop of Down and Connor 1982–90, Archbishop of Armagh and Primate of all Ireland 1990–6

Edward Daly (1933–2016), priest who was present during Bloody Sunday, February 1972; bishop of Derry 1974–94

General John de Chastelain, Canadian armed forces 1996–8, one of the international chairmen overseeing talks that led to Good Friday Agreement, Member of Independent International Commission on Decommissioning

Éamon de Valera (1882–1975), taoiseach 1932–48, 1951–4, 1957–9; president of Ireland 1959–73

Pat Doherty, vice-president of Sinn Féin 1988–2009, member of Northern Ireland Assembly 1998–2017

Alf Dubs, British Labour MP 1979–87, life peer 1997, parliamentary under-secretary at Northern Ireland Office 1997–9

Robin Eames, Church of Ireland archbishop of Armagh and Primate of all Ireland 1986–2009

David Ervine (1953–2007), member of Northern Ireland Assembly 1998–2007, leader of Progressive Unionist Party 2002–7

Ronan Fanning (1941–2017), professor of modern history, University College Dublin 1985–2007

Sean Farrell, Department of Foreign Affairs

Fr Denis Faul (1932–2006), priest and civil rights campaigner

Brian Faulkner (1921–77), last prime minister of Northern Ireland (1971–2), chief executive of the Northern Ireland Executive 1974

Sir Nicholas Fenn, UK ambassador to Ireland 1986–91

Desmond Fennell, writer and commentator

Garret FitzGerald (1926–2011), minister for foreign affairs 1973–77, leader of Fine Gael 1977–87, taoiseach 1981–2, 1982–7

Pádraig Flynn, Fianna Fáil TD 1977–94, minister for justice 1993–4, EU commissioner 1993–9

George Foulkes, British Labour MP 1979–2005

Sir Marcus Fox (1927–2002), Conservative MP 1970–97, vice-chair (1983–94) and chair (1994–7) of 1922 Committee of backbench Conservative MPs

Dermot Gallagher (1944–2017), Irish ambassador to the USA 1991–7, second secretary at Department of the Taoiseach 1997–9, key role in Good Friday Agreement, secretary general of Department of the Taoiseach 2000–2, secretary general of Department of Foreign Affairs 2002–9

Eamonn Gallagher (1926–2009), Department of Foreign Affairs, EU official

Dermot Gleeson, attorney general 1994–7

Robin Glendinning, founding member of Alliance Party of Northern Ireland

David Goodall (1931–2016), deputy-secretary Cabinet Office, deputy under-secretary Foreign Office 1982–7

Ian Gow (1937–90), Conservative MP 1974–90, parliamentary private secretary to Prime Minister Thatcher, assassinated by Provisional IRA

Grey Gowrie, Scottish hereditary peer, born Dublin; Conservative politician

Baron Hailsham (1907–2001), Conservative politician, lord chancellor 1970–4, 1979–87

Mary Harney, TD 1981–2002, tánaiste 1997–2006, leader of Progressive Democrats 1993–2006

Roy Hattersley, British Labour MP 1964–97; deputy leader of Labour 1983–92

Charles Haughey (1925–2006), Fianna Fáil TD 1957–92; Cabinet minister 1961–70, 1977–9; leader of Fianna Fáil 1979–92; taoiseach 1979–81, 1982, 1987–92

Ted Heath, Conservative politician, British prime minister 1970–4

Joe Hendron, SDLP politician

Jack Hermon (1928–2008), chief constable of RUC 1980–9

Patrick Hillery (1923–2008), Fianna Fáil TD 1951–73, minister for external affairs 1969–73, EEC commissioner 1973–6, president of Ireland 1976–90

John Holmes, UK diplomat, private secretary and principal private secretary to prime minister 1995–9

Geoffrey Howe (1926–2015), Conservative MP 1974–92, foreign secretary 1983–9

John Hume, founding member SDLP, leader 1979–2001; member Northern Ireland Parliament 1969–72, European Parliament

1979–2004, UK Parliament 1983–2005, Northern Ireland Assembly (1998–2000); Nobel Peace Prize winner 1998

Douglas Hurd, Conservative MP 1974–7, secretary of state for Northern Ireland 1984–5, home secretary 1985–9, foreign secretary 1989–95

Edward Kennedy (1932–2000), senator for Massachusetts 1962–2009, one of the Four Horsemen

Tom King, Conservative politician, secretary of state for Northern Ireland 1985–9

Neil Kinnock, leader of British Labour Party 1983–92

Wally Kirwan, Department of the Taoiseach

Julia Langdon, British journalist

Seán Lemass (1899–1971), Fianna Fáil TD 1927–66, taoiseach 1959–66

Brian Lenihan (1930–95), Fianna Fáil TD 1961–73, 1977–95; tánaiste and minister for foreign affairs 1987–9

Hugh Logue, member of Northern Ireland Civil Rights Association, SDLP politician, member of New Ireland Forum

Lord Lowry (1919–99), lord chief justice of Northern Ireland 1971–88, chair of Northern Ireland Constitutional Convention 1975

Jack Lynch (1917–99), Fianna Fáil TD 1948–81, taoiseach 1966–73, 1977–9

Alistair McAlpine (1942–2014), treasurer of Conservative Party 1979–90

Seán MacBride (1904–88), leader of Clann na Poblachta 1948–65, minister for external affairs 1951–4, Nobel Peace Prize winner 1974, Lenin Peace Prize winner 1975–6, author of 'MacBride principles' relating to employment discrimination in Northern Ireland

Robert McCartney, unionist politician, expelled from UUP 1987, founder/leader of UK Unionist Party 1995–2008, Westminster MP 1995–2001, member of Northern Ireland Assembly 1998–2007

John McColgan, Department of Foreign Affairs

Bob McDonagh, Department of Foreign Affairs

Christopher McGimpsey, UUP politician, member of Northern Ireland Assembly 1998–2016

Michael McGimpsey, UUP politician, member of Northern Ireland Assembly 1998–2016

P.J. McGrory, Belfast solicitor

Tomás Mac Giolla (1924–2010), leader of (sequentially) Sinn Féin, Official Sinn Féin, Sinn Féin—the Workers' Party and the Workers' Party 1962–88; TD 1982–92

Eddie McGrady (1935–2013), nationalist politician, founding member of SDLP, Westminster MP 1987–2010, member of Northern Ireland Assembly 1998–2003

Martin McGuinness (1950–2017), prominent member of Provisional IRA and Sinn Féin, deputy first minister of Northern Ireland 2007–17

Eamonn McKee, Department of Foreign Affairs

Mitchel McLaughlin, general secretary of Sinn Féin, member of Northern Ireland Assembly 1998–2016

Kevin McNamara (1924–2017), British Labour Party spokesman on Northern Ireland 1984–97

Rev. Roy Magee, Presbyterian minister, intermediary between the Combined Loyalist Military Command and the Irish and British governments

John Major, prime minister and Conservative Party leader 1990–7, MP 1979–2001

Seamus Mallon, deputy leader of SDLP 1979–2001, deputy first minister of Northern Ireland 1998–2001

Roy Mason (1924–2015), British Labour politician, defence secretary 1974–6, secretary of state for Northern Ireland 1976–9

Patrick (Paddy) Mayhew (1929–2016), Conservative MP 1974–97, secretary of state for Northern Ireland 1992–7

George Mitchell, United States special envoy for Northern Ireland 1995–2001

James Molyneaux (Baron Molyneaux of Killead) (1920–2015), leader of Ulster Unionist Party 1974–96

Mo Mowlam (1949–2005), British Labour MP 1987–2001, secretary of state for Northern Ireland 1997–9

Daniel Patrick Moynihan (1927–2003), US senator for New York State 1977–2001, another of the Four Horsemen

Fr Raymond Murray, priest of archdiocese of Armagh, champion of republican prisoners

Paul Murphy, British Labour MP 1987–2015, secretary of state for Northern Ireland 2002–5

Dermot Nally (1927–2009) Department of the Taoiseach, assistant secretary 1973–78, deputy-secretary 1978–80, secretary 1980–92

Airey Neave (1916–79), Conservative MP 1953–79; shadow secretary of state for Northern Ireland; assassinated by INLA bomb fitted to his car, which detonated at Westminster

Richard Needham, Conservative MP 1979–97, under-secretary of state for Northern Ireland 1985–92

Tauno Nieminen, brigadier-general in Finnish Army, member of Independent International Commission on Decommissioning

Conor Cruise O'Brien (1917–2008), diplomat, writer, Labour TD 1969–77, minister for posts and telegraphs 1973–7

Dáithí Ó Conaill (1938–91), member of Provisional IRA army council and vice-president of Sinn Féin; broke with Sinn Féin in 1986, becoming chairman of Republican Sinn Féin

Liz O'Donnell, Progressive Democrat TD 1992–2007, minister of state at Department of Foreign Affairs 1997–2002

Declan O'Donovan, Department of Foreign Affairs

Philip (Paddy) O'Donoghue (1896–1987), judge of the European Court of Human Rights

Cardinal Tomas Ó Fiaich (1923–90), Roman Catholic archbishop of Armagh and primate of all Ireland, 1977–90

Paddy O'Hanlon (1944–2009), Northern Ireland MP 1969–72, founding member of SDLP

Colm Ó hEocha (1926–97), president of University College Galway 1975–97, chairman of New Ireland Forum 1983–4

Des O'Malley, Fianna Fáil politician, founder and first leader of Progressive Democrats, minister for justice 1970–73

Terence O'Neill (1914–90), prime minister of Northern Ireland and leader of Ulster Unionist Party 1963–9

Tip O'Neill (1912–94), Speaker of US House of Representatives 1977–87, Democratic Party politician, one of the Four Horsemen

Ian Paisley (1926–2014), founder of Democratic Unionist Party 1971, leader 1971–2008, first minister of Northern Ireland Assembly 2007–8

Charles Powell, private secretary to Margaret Thatcher 1983–90 and John Major 1990–1

Enoch Powell, Conservative MP 1950–74; Ulster Unionist Party MP for South Down 1974–87

Jonathan Powell, chief of staff to Tony Blair and chief negotiator on Northern Ireland 1997–2007

Jim Prior, Conservative secretary of state for Northern Ireland 1981–4

Declan Quigley, legal official in the office of the attorney general

Cyril Ramaphosa, South African politician, member of Independent International Commission on Decommissioning 2000–1, president of South Africa 2018–

Gordon Reece, journalist, media expert and adviser to prime minister Margaret Thatcher

Merlyn Rees, British Labour MP, secretary of state for Northern Ireland 1974–6, home secretary 1976–9

Fr Alec Reid (1931–2013), Redemptorist priest based in Clonard Monastery, Belfast; a key intermediary between Sinn Féin/IRA and Irish and British governments

Albert Reynolds (1932–2014), taoiseach and leader of Fianna Fáil 1992–4

Mary Robinson, president of Ireland 1990–7, senator 1969–89

Brid Rogers, Involved in Civil Rights Movement, founding member of SDLP, minister for agriculture and rural development, Northern Ireland, 1999–2002

George Seawright (1951–87), unionist politician and paramilitary, assassinated 1987 by Irish People's Liberation Organisation

Andy Sens, former US diplomat, member of staff of Independent International Commission on Decommissioning

Clare Short, Labour MP 1983–2006, independent MP 2006–10, member of Blair Cabinet 1997–2003

Joe Small, Department of Foreign Affairs

Clive Soley, Labour MP 1979–2005

Gusty Spence (1933–2011), leader of paramilitary Ulster Volunteer Force; convicted in 1966 for the murder of Peter Ward, a Catholic; released from prison in 1984; became a member of the Progressive Unionist Party and a key figure in the peace process.

Dick Spring, leader of Irish Labour Party 1982–97, tánaiste and minister for foreign affairs 1994–7

Ivor Stanbrook (1924–2004), Conservative MP 1970–92

Jim Steinberg, deputy national security advisor to US President Bill Clinton 1996–2000

Sir Ninian Stephen (1923–2017), Australian judge and governor-general of Australia, chairman of Anglo-Irish strand of Northern Ireland peace talks 1992

John Swift, Department of Foreign Affairs

John Taylor, unionist politician, member of Northern Ireland parliament 1965–72, Westminster MP 1983–2001, member of Northern Ireland Assembly 1998–2007, deputy leader of Ulster Unionist Party 1998–2007

Norman Tebbit, Conservative MP and Cabinet minister; his wife was seriously injured in 1984 Brighton bombing

Peter Temple-Morris (1938–2018), MP 1970–2001; Conservative, joined Labour Party 1998

Margaret Thatcher (1925–2013), British prime minister 1979–90

David Trimble (Baron Trimble), leader of Ulster Unionist Party 1995–2005, first minister of Northern Ireland 1998–2002, Nobel Peace Prize winner 1998

Andrew (Andy) Ward (1926–99), secretary of Department of Justice 1971–86

T.K. Whitaker (1916–2017), secretary of Department of Finance, governor of the Central Bank, key contact behind the first meeting between Taoiseach Seán Lemass and Northern Ireland Prime Minister Terence O'Neill, adviser on Northern Ireland to Taoiseach Jack Lynch

William (Willie) Whitelaw (1918–99), Conservative politician, MP 1954–83, House of Lords 1983–99, first secretary of state for Northern Ireland

Shirley Williams, British Labour politician and founding member of Social Democratic Party

Harold Wilson (1916–95), British Labour politician, prime minister 1964–70 and 1974–6

John Wilson (1923–2007), Fianna Fáil TD 1973–99, tánaiste 1990–3; Irish Victims' Commissioner

Larry Wren (1922–2016), commissioner of an Garda Síochána 1983–7

Billy Wright (1960–97), Ulster loyalist leader, murdered in Maze Prison 1997

Foreword

OLIVIA O'LEARY

I was sitting at dinner in the British ambassador's residence in Glencairn when the ambassador began to talk to me about certain officials in the Department of Foreign Affairs.* There was one in particular he was finding it tough to deal with.

'You know this man O hUiginn?', he asked. 'The one they call the Prince of Darkness?'

'Isn't he brilliant?', I countered. 'A true mandarin. We're very, very proud of him.' The ambassador immediately turned to talk to the guest on his other side.

Journalists and government officials don't always see eye to eye: we do different jobs. But no Irish person was going to put up with the representative of a foreign government criticising an Irish official for doing his job. Most British ambassadors to Ireland would have been more careful. And while officials usually work well away from the public gaze, those of us covering Northern Ireland over the years saw enough to make us appreciate what sensitive and vital work Irish civil servants were doing, and how seriously they took it.

It's hard for anybody born in the past 30 years to appreciate how the outbreak of the Troubles affected society in the Republic.

---

*Please note that Department of External Affairs was the official title until 1973, when it was changed to Department of Foreign Affairs. For convenience, Department of Foreign Affairs (DFA) is used throughout this book.

Cycling through Bagenalstown in County Carlow as a local reporter in 1971, I heard speakers at a public meeting in the square openly urging people to join the IRA. Civil war passions came to the surface again, and Jack Lynch sacked members of his own cabinet for an alleged attempt to import arms. All this was sprung on a society that hadn't thought much about Northern Ireland for decades. De Valera's attitude to the border was that Britain created it, so Britain should get rid of it. Even though Seán Lemass had made that historic trip to Northern Ireland to meet Terence O'Neill in 1965, policy on the north hadn't developed much beyond anti-partitionism. Indeed, in 1969, as Noel Dorr has pointed out in his fine book on Sunningdale, neither the Department of Foreign Affairs nor the Department of the Taoiseach had a section or even an individual assigned specifically to the Northern Ireland issue.

What's more, we had not tried to find a way to talk to the British about Northern Ireland. It was always going to be a touchy issue, but two grown-up states should have found a grown-up way to communicate with one another even over disputed territory. Instead we had telegrams at dawn between Jack Lynch and Edward Heath in August 1971 when internment was introduced. Lynch protested at a continued policy of what he called military solutions, and said he would now support the non-unionist population's campaign of passive resistance. Heath retorted angrily that it was unacceptable that Lynch should try to interfere in the affairs of Northern Ireland. Lynch replied: 'Mr Heath's assertion that what is happening in Northern Ireland is no concern of mine is not acceptable. The division of Ireland has never been, and is not now, acceptable to the great majority of the Irish people.'

Then our bishop, Paddy Lennon, got in on the act and, from the pulpit of Carlow Cathedral, declared that what Heath said was petulant, arrogant and patently untrue, since what happened in Northern Ireland was our business as Irish people and as Christians. I remember it well because it was the first news story I ever had printed in a national newspaper, *The Irish Times*.

It shocked me that senior statesmen should resort to catcalling across the Irish Sea—brawling in public, as the then British ambassador, Sir John Peck, called it. However, from reading Noel Dorr's book, I now know that Lynch's insistence on asserting Ireland's right to interfere back then in August 1971 had come on the advice of Eamonn Gallagher in Foreign Affairs, and that, far from alienating the British, Lynch's assertiveness meant that within months, Ted Heath was including him in talks at Chequers with Brian Faulkner. So they finally decided to be mature: to sit down and talk about it. We have benefited enormously since from that realisation by both governments: that they were much stronger working together on Northern Ireland than remaining hostage to their respective extremists. It served us well, despite a few wobbles right through to the Good Friday Agreement of 1998.

But there were no easy steps along that way. Back in the early 1970s, the view was still held in certain quarters that Ireland, in asserting its right to interfere, had to be ready for conflict; that militant unionists would have to be confronted by arms if necessary. However, it was clear that wiser council was prevailing when Jack Lynch established the principle of no change in the status of Northern Ireland without unionist consent when he wrote an article, as Seán Donlon points out, for the prestigious US *Foreign Policy* journal in 1972. This was despite the provocation of the Bloody Sunday killings in Derry earlier that year by the British army.

Watching from the sidelines over the following three decades, I could see again and again that progress in Northern Ireland was made when the British and Irish governments were in cooperative contact with one another, and no progress was made when they were not. I remember at Sunningdale being conscious of the effort being made by British premier Ted Heath to use his power and his presence to ensure these talks would succeed. The ease with which Liam Cosgrave and Brian Faulkner, both hunting men, seemed to get on showed the vital importance of face-to-face meetings. And the give wasn't all on the unionist side. The SDLP's press conference after the Sunningdale Agreement was made uncomfortable as Austin Currie was heckled again and again by a reporter from the north who reminded him that he said he would never agree to a settlement while internment continued. Currie was one of the bravest and brightest of the SDLP representatives, but compromise was asked for from all sides and it would be 1975 before internment was finished for good.

We had such great hopes for that power-sharing executive. It was after all the first time that nationalists had been allowed into government in the north. There were various stories of nationalist ministers on their first day in the office. SDLP minister Paddy Devlin told me that on his first day, he called in all his senior officials and told them that he was deeply concerned about the lack of balance in the department's staff—that it was discriminatory and he was going to do something about it. All around him, he said, faces of the mainly Protestant officials went pale. 'We need more …', said Paddy, milking the moment—'We need more women!'

It was obvious that certain moderate unionist ministers such as Basil McIvor, and indeed Brian Faulkner himself, did their best to make the executive work. But continued republican violence, and lack of support from some unionist ministers in the executive, from some senior officials, and eventually from the new Labour government in Britain under Harold Wilson, led to the success of the Ulster Workers' Council strike and the fall of the executive.

There was chaos in the north. Constant power cuts meant that the sewerage system stopped working, and in the corridors of Belfast's Europa hotel, where I was staying, you could smell defeat.

As a young reporter, I did the only thing I could think of doing. I stood beside a British army officer on the Malone Road in Belfast as a loyalist mob pushed hijacked cars and vans together to form a barricade blocking the road. 'They're breaking the law. Aren't you going to stop them? Why won't you stop them?', I badgered him. He refused to answer and suggested that I buzz off, that it wasn't safe for me to be there, and that it was none of my business. I stood there for an hour embarrassing him, but with my mouth as dry as sawdust because as an Irish person I knew I was watching the British powers-that-be allowing the only real attempt at consensus government in Northern Ireland to disappear down the drain—or indeed the sewer.

Yet I knew too that for the Irish government, rebuilding the relationship with the unionist community and with the British government was the only way forward. When Ireland had the EEC presidency in 1975, Garret FitzGerald as foreign minister did his best to meet with his British counterpart on the margin of European meetings. He made a particular point of calling on the new opposition leader, Margaret Thatcher, whenever he was in London on European business, and it was a courtesy she did not forget when she became prime minister.

Things did not go so well with Taoiseach Charles Haughey, despite his attempt to put Anglo-Irish relations on a new footing with his 'totality of relations' approach and the suggestion that Ireland might be ready to join NATO as part of a settlement on Northern Ireland. Once again, the British accused the Irish of over-selling the possibility of achieving Irish unity from the talks.

I knew it was all over when I woke in Buenos Aires one early May morning in 1982 to hear every news bulletin beginning with the words: *Señor Paddy Power, el ministro de las fuerzas armadas de Irlanda … Señor Paddy Power … Señor Paddy Power…*

I was in Argentina covering the Falklands War, or, as they called it, La Guerra de las Malvinas, and Argentina was crowing over Ireland's action. The Argentine reports said that after the sinking by Britain of the Argentine cruiser *General Belgrano*, with the loss of 323 sailors' lives, on 2 May, doughty Kildare man and defence minister Paddy Power had said that Britain should get out of the Falklands and they should get out of our island too. When I checked the Irish newspapers, they reported Power as having been more restrained, saying that the sinking of the *Belgrano*, outside the British-declared total exclusion zone, suggested to him that Britain was now the aggressor in the Falklands war.

Two days after the sinking, Haughey announced that Ireland would be pulling out of the EEC sanctions against Argentina. Suddenly Ireland was *numero uno* in Buenos Aires. I was granted a rare interview with the Argentine chancellor, Nicanor Costa Mendes. Meanwhile in Britain, Margaret Thatcher was so angry that she was exploring the removal of voting rights from an estimated 500,000 citizens of the Republic living in the UK. The Irish Exporters Association told Haughey that the trade 'backlash' in the UK because of Ireland's policy of opposing EEC sanctions was 'the most severe since at least 1969'.

Sales of Paddy Power whiskey may have boomed in Argentina, but we had managed to become best friends with one of the nastiest and most murderous military dictatorships in the world at the cost of our friendship with the neighbour from whom we most needed cooperation on Northern Ireland.

The road built from here to the Anglo-Irish agreement of 1985 was a massive achievement not only for Garret FitzGerald but for a whole cadre of Irish officials and diplomats. I remember doing a television profile of Garret FitzGerald for the BBC at the time and following him into the Burlington Hotel one day, where people in the lobby spontaneously stood up and cheered. Ireland for the first time had a consultative role in the affairs of Northern Ireland. People were delighted. The same people threw him out of government in 1987. A taoiseach who presides over record unemployment and the worst emigration record since the 1950s doesn't get re-elected, regardless of his record on the north.

The road to the ceasefires of the 1990s and to the Good Friday/Belfast Agreement marked a whole other chapter in which successive taoisigh played their part, and I was glad to see the generous tribute paid to Albert Reynolds, despite their past disagreements, in Fergus Finlay's piece for this book. But Haughey played a part too, not only in allowing the first tentative contacts to be made with the republican movement but in working the Anglo-Irish Agreement he had condemned while in opposition. The close contacts between the British and Irish governments continued over that very difficult period—difficult because violence continued despite the fact that the republican movement was looking for a deal.

Crucial to that Irish–British relationship were the contacts and even friendships between British and Irish officials who had got to know one another at senior level and in the pressure-cooker atmosphere that must have prevailed in the Maryfield bunker. Civil servants have the advantage of being the permanent government, so their friendships and good relationships can last much longer than those between politicians. I was commuting to work in London in the mid-1980s, and regularly filed on to the early Aer Lingus plane back to Dublin with Sir Robert Armstrong and his colleagues. It was a reassuring feeling that people of this calibre were on the job, trying to deal with an ongoing problem that hurt us all.

But the difference between civil servants and journalists was brought home to me once more when I was working for BBC's *Newsnight* in London in that mid-1980s period. The then Irish ambassador to the UK, Noel Dorr, asked me to lunch at the embassy in Grosvenor Place. Over lunch I confided to him that I was going to return to Ireland in a few months' time. He did not approve. He pointed out to me gently but firmly how important it was for Ireland to have an Irish person in a prominent position in the British media at that crucial time. I had never thought of myself in that light. I'm a journalist. My duty is to the people I broadcast to or write for, to the truth of any story in as far as I can see it. My sense of duty was different from his.

But I admired his total commitment to his country and his country's good. I admire all those who stayed up all night redrafting documents, or who found the new phrase that would oil the wheels of a crucial negotiation next day. I admire those who walked the streets and back lanes of Belfast and Derry when it was really dangerous, who talked to contacts on all sides to make sure that the Irish government could make informed decisions. I admire those who networked and lunched for Ireland way beyond their boredom threshold and won over unlikely allies. I admire those who were brave enough to give unwelcome advice when it would have been much easier to say nothing.

Some of them have told their stories, many for the first time, in this series of revealing essays. They served their country—our country—well. We should be grateful.

Introduction

MARY E. DALY

On 22 March 2018 the Royal Irish Academy hosted a remarkable one-day conference, where many of the Irish public servants who worked on the Northern Ireland peace process from the late 1960s until the 1998 Good Friday Agreement spoke about their involvement in that lengthy process. This book brings these contributions to a wider audience.

Some had told their story on other occasions that are captured in various books, journal articles, archives and films. The John Whyte oral archive—which holds material on British–Irish and Northern Irish negotiations between 1972 and 2006—in University College Dublin Archives, which was released in April 2018, contains 34 interviews with politicians and public servants, but Richard Ryan is the only one of the contributors to this book to feature in that collection. (The archive was developed by UCD professors John Coakley and Jennifer Todd. A list of the interviewees and the background to the collection can be found at: https://www.ucd.ie/archives/collections/depositedcollections/. Transcripts of the interviews can be consulted by appointment at UCD Archives.) There are many other first-hand accounts by politicians, political advisers and public servants of their involvement in the Northern Ireland peace process, and some include comments by the contributors to this book, but this is the first work that concentrates exclusively on the role of Irish civil servants and political advisers in the Northern Ireland peace process.

All those involved with the March 2018 conference were conscious that ultimately the Good Friday Agreement was delivered by politicians, and the evolution of Irish policy on Northern Ireland was also determined by politicians. The public servants and political advisers whose experiences are captured in this book worked in a highly sensitive political environment, subject to political oversight, but that does not detract from the importance attached to their work. Their contributions evoke a strong sense of that environment and the impact of an ever-changing political landscape—in Britain, the United States and Ireland—on prospects for advancing the Northern Ireland peace process.

The aim of both the conference and this book is not to celebrate the Good Friday Agreement, but rather to reflect on the evolution of policy and thinking about Northern Ireland over the 30 years from the outbreak of violence in 1968 to the conclusion of the 1998 agreement. These contributions show that the Good Friday Agreement was not inevitable: that it was hard-won. They also reveal the persistent effort that was required of Irish politicians and public servants to secure a role for Ireland in resolving the Northern Ireland conflict, and the critical changes in Irish policy and attitudes that were necessary to give due recognition and respect to the unionist tradition.

The outbreak of violence in Northern Ireland in 1968 was arguably the greatest challenge for the Irish government since independence, even greater than neutrality in the Second World War. It led to an immediate need to develop policy towards Northern Ireland, establish appropriate administrative structures, gather information and interject an Irish voice into media coverage. A new word emerged within the Irish civil service: 'travellers'—the Irish officials who spent so much time in Northern Ireland meeting people from both unionist and nationalist traditions, and reporting back to Dublin. Irish public servants, working closely with John Hume, helped to build a key Irish-American political lobby that counteracted the traditionally Anglophile US State Department. A long series of meetings, and close personal relationships between Irish and British officials, paved the way for the 1985

Anglo-Irish Agreement signed by Taoiseach Garret FitzGerald and Prime Minister Margaret Thatcher, and the massive majority in Westminster that voted in favour of that agreement was at least partly due to the dedicated efforts of Irish diplomats to educate British MPs about Northern Ireland. The book also captures the sacrifices in terms of family and personal life, and the distinct role played by political advisers. It recalls the Forum for a New Ireland, which represented the first serious reflection since independence about Irish unity, partition and identities, and the importance of the Brooke–Mayhew talks: two episodes that have receded from popular memory.

At an early stage in planning the Academy conference, it became evident that the list of probable speakers was exclusively male. It would have been otherwise if we had extended the contributors to include politicians—Máire Geoghegan Quinn and Liz O'Donnell played key roles in the Downing Street Agreement and Good Friday Agreement respectively, and Monica McWilliams of the Northern Ireland Women's Party was an active participant in both the negotiations leading up to the Good Friday Agreement and the 2018 Academy conference. Women will feature in future conferences and volumes that bring the story up to the 2006 St Andrews Agreement and beyond. Their absence on this occasion reflects historical reality: until 1973 all women civil servants had to resign on marriage, a rule that seriously depleted the pool of talent in the Irish public service. It is also evident that service in Northern Ireland was regarded as dangerous, and therefore women might not have been selected for these roles. In order to partially address this gender imbalance, the four sessions at the Academy conference were moderated by women: Dr Margaret O'Callaghan of Queen's University Belfast; Catherine Day, former secretary general of the European Commission; Ireland's ambassador to Mexico Barbara Jones, who has significant experience of working on Northern Ireland and British–Irish relations post 1998; and myself. Each moderator has contributed a short reflection on the panel that she chaired. The foreword is supplied by Olivia O'Leary, one of the pioneering women journalists who covered the Northern Ireland Troubles.

My thanks go to all the contributors to this book for agreeing to put their stories in the record, and to all who participated in the

Academy conference and contributed their knowledge from the floor. The audience included many people who were also involved in this story. Many speakers recalled their former colleagues. The late Dermot Gallagher, former secretary general of the Department of Foreign Affairs, was mentioned in every session. We had hoped that Frank Murray, former secretary to the government, would join us on the day, but he was ill and died shortly after the conference.

The other absent giant who featured throughout the conference was John Hume. He was the initial point of contact for Irish officials trying to develop a knowledge of Northern Ireland, and he was also instrumental in building critical connections with US politicians—a development that proved critical in securing the 1998 Good Friday Agreement.

The conference would not have been possible without the assistance of the Department of Foreign Affairs and Trade, who helped to identify possible speakers and attendees. My thanks go to Tánaiste and Minister for Foreign Affairs and Trade Simon Coveney; to Secretary General Niall Burgess and to Eoghan Duffy and Fionnuala Callanan for advice and assistance. My thanks go also to the president, council and staff of the Royal Irish Academy for supporting the conference, and to the RIA's outstanding publications office, especially Ruth Hegarty, Helena King and Fidelma Slattery.

Early Stages
to the
New Ireland Forum

—

The Rocky Road to the Good Friday Agreement

SEÁN DONLON

Much of my career in the Department of Foreign Affairs (1963–87) and the Department of the Taoiseach (1994–7) involved dealing with matters related to Northern Ireland. In my various roles in Ireland, north and south, in the United States and on the many trips to London, I saw at first hand the dramatic changes that took place in the 30 years from the start of the Troubles to the signing of the Good Friday Agreement.

In the early days, relations between Dublin and London were poor. London took the view that Northern Ireland was none of Dublin's business. In 1971 British prime minister Ted Heath told the taoiseach, Jack Lynch, in response to proposals he had made, that his attempts to interfere 'in the affairs of the United Kingdom' were unacceptable. Appeals to the US were similarly rebuffed. The US position, formulated by the State Department, slavishly reflected the UK view.

By the time of the Good Friday Agreement 30 years later, Dublin, London and Washington were singing from the same hymn sheet. And the situation in Northern Ireland had changed. One-party unionist rule was gone and power-sharing was in.

Much had changed in all three capitals. London realised that acting alone, it could not hope to achieve peace and stability in Northern Ireland. In Washington, under pressure from prominent Irish-American politicians, the US came to the view that it could play a role helpful to both the UK and Ireland. In Dublin the main political parties moved to a fundamentally new policy, one that was significantly inspired by John Hume. It was more realistic and less aspirational than the one that had prevailed since the foundation of the state.

This chapter attempts to throw some light on the following themes, which are relevant background to the long, twisty and bumpy road to the Good Friday Agreement:

- the development of Irish government policy
- the emergence of civil service structures to deal with Northern Ireland matters
- the Strasbourg case
- Anglo-Irish relations in the 1970s
- US involvement.

DEVELOPMENT OF IRISH GOVERNMENT POLICY

Donal Barrington was the first person to question publicly the sterile de Valera policy: that Britain had partitioned Ireland and it was its responsibility to undo partition. In his 1957 Tuairim pamphlet *Uniting Ireland* and his subsequent article of the same name in *Studies* (1957: 46, pp 379–402), his central theme was that partition was not forced on Ireland by Britain but was necessitated by the conflicting demands of two groups of Irish people, unionists and nationalists. John Hume's position, to which he remained loyal throughout his political life, was set out in articles in *The Irish Times* on 18/19 May 1964. The three principles underlying his agenda were: a rejection of violence, that there could be no Irish unity without the consent of the Northern Ireland majority, and that there had to be a recognition that nationalism was an acceptable political belief and that people in Northern Ireland and elsewhere were entitled to advocate it and work towards achieving its goals. Garret FitzGerald broadly supported these principles in his 1964 *Studies* article 'Seeking a national purpose' (53, pp 337–51).

With the outbreak of the Troubles in Northern Ireland in late 1968, the Irish government was under pressure to respond. The Seán Lemass/Terence O'Neill meetings in 1965 had broken the Dublin/Belfast ice but within Northern Ireland discrimination in jobs, housing and electoral arrangements remained. The devolved government in Stormont was exclusively unionist and London turned a blind eye to domestic affairs in Northern Ireland.

It took a while for a statement of Dublin's policy to emerge. The taoiseach, Jack Lynch, set out government policy in a speech in Tralee in September 1969, which was drafted by T.K. Whitaker. Lynch emphasised that there could be 'no change in the status of Northern Ireland without the consent of a majority'. But it quickly became clear that there were dissenting opinions within the government, notably on the role of violence. It was only when dissident ministers resigned or were removed from office in May 1970 that a clear policy began to emerge. Violence was rejected and the principle of no change in the status of Northern Ireland without unionist consent was generally accepted. In an article drafted by Noel Dorr and Eamonn Gallagher of the Department of Foreign Affairs, published in the July 1972 issue of the US journal *Foreign Policy*, Jack Lynch removed any doubts that remained about government policy. By that stage both Fine Gael and the Labour Party had adopted broadly similar policies.

CIVIL SERVICE STRUCTURES

At the outbreak of the Troubles neither the Department of the Taoiseach nor the Department of Foreign Affairs was structured to deal with the situation. No person or section in either department was tasked with a Northern Ireland brief. The absence of detailed, reliable information about what was happening in Northern Ireland, combined with the lack of clarity on policy, created particular difficulties for official representatives abroad. Requests for information or instructions went unanswered or were met with that well-known civil service reply, 'whatever you say, say nothing'. To satisfy a domestic audience the government had to be seen to be doing something. A number of publicity initiatives were taken in 1969, including the appointment of press officers from semi-state bodies to key diplomatic missions, and the appointment of a Geneva-based public relations firm, Markpress. These efforts were, however, largely ineffective, again because of the lack of clarity on policy and the absence of back-up civil service structures.

That was the background against which a middle-level official in the Department of Foreign Affairs, Eamonn Gallagher, began to apply his professional skills. Without seeking the approval of the department or initially revealing what he was doing, he established contact with John Hume in Derry in August 1969, and through him, with others who were actively involved politically or as community leaders. Many of these people went on to create and launch the Social Democratic and Labour Party (SDLP) in August 1970. Gallagher travelled regularly in Northern Ireland, usually in his own time at weekends, in a somewhat distinctive, battered left-hand-drive Renault 4 that he had imported on his transfer from the embassy in Paris. Personal security was not high on his agenda! On the basis of the information gleaned from his contacts, he prepared reports analysing the situation and making policy recommendations. These were submitted to the secretary of the department, who forwarded them to the minister, Dr Patrick Hillery and the taoiseach, Jack Lynch.

Early in 1970 a Northern Ireland unit was established within the department's political division and Gallagher, with the rank of counsellor, was appointed as its head. Joe Small joined subsequently as a first secretary and there were two third secretaries and supporting clerical staff.

It was not until February 1972 that a totally new division was created in the department and allocated responsibility for Northern Ireland, international press and information, and cultural affairs. It was headed by an assistant secretary, initially Bob McDonagh. I held the position from 1974 to 1978. Administratively the Department of the Taoiseach continued to have responsibility for policy on Northern Ireland, with the Department of Foreign Affairs responsible for feeding into policy formulation and implementing the policy that emerged. With the appointment in 1972 of Dermot

Nally as an assistant secretary in the Department of the Taoiseach and the subsequent appointment of Wally Kirwan to assist him, there were two departments reasonably equipped to advise on the increasingly difficult situation in Northern Ireland. Matters relating to the security of the state and north–south security cooperation remained in the Department of Justice. The Department of Defence also had a security role, though it took some time for that department to re-establish its credibility after the fallout from the arms trial and related events in 1969/70.

THE STRASBOURG CASE

In August 1971 I was recalled from my position as consul-general in Boston to go to Northern Ireland to investigate the circumstances surrounding the introduction of internment without trial. I was assured that the assignment would take two or three months. I ended up spending much of the next seven years in Northern Ireland!

Reports reaching the department suggested that in the introduction of internment, the focus had been exclusively on the minority nationalist community. It also emerged that a number of those interned had been subject to particularly cruel and harsh interrogation techniques. There were widespread complaints about the general behaviour of the security forces. My task was to assemble as much information as possible to provide a basis for the government's reaction. Within a matter of weeks, on the basis of statements from internees with supporting medical evidence, a pattern of 'interrogation in depth' was established. Twelve of the approximately 350 men lifted in dawn raids on 11 August had been subjected to it. Two others followed in October. The treatment involved, *inter alia*, hooding, standing in search positions for extended periods, sleep deprivation, exposure to high-pitched noise for up to six days, physical brutality and deprivation of food and drink.

I was hugely assisted in my task by Fr Brian Brady and the Association for Legal Justice in Belfast, Fr Denis Faul in Dungannon and Fr Raymond Murray in Armagh, together with a number of solicitors, doctors and community leaders. The Central Citizens Defence Committee in Belfast, under the leadership of Canon Padraig Murphy and Tom Conaty, was also very helpful.

On the basis of the material assembled, the Irish government raised the matter with the UK government and, failing to get a satisfactory response, decided to take a case to the European Commission and Court of Human Rights in Strasbourg. In 1976 the Commission found (Ireland v UK, 1976 European Commission of Human Rights, Rts 512, 748, 788–94) that the behaviour of the security forces amounted to torture. On appeal, the court in 1978 overturned that decision (case 5310/71) and ruled that it amounted to inhuman and degrading treatment, but not torture. In 2013, on the basis of newly released and declassified UK documents, the government reopened the case but the decision that torture was not involved was confirmed.

We now know, on the basis of released UK papers (for example a letter from the UK home secretary, Merlyn Rees, to his prime minister, James Callaghan, in 1977), that the interrogation techniques had been specifically authorised by UK ministers, in particular the then Secretary of State for Defence, Peter Carrington. In 1977, in the course of the Ireland v UK court case, the then UK attorney general gave 'an unqualified undertaking that the "five techniques" used in Northern Ireland in 1971 would not in any circumstances be reintroduced as an aid to interrogation'.

As far as the British were concerned, the Strasbourg case was an irritant in Anglo-Irish relations from 1971 to 1978, but the government—in particular the minister for foreign affairs, Garret FitzGerald, and the attorney general, Declan Costello—saw the case in a wider international human rights context and pursued it in the hope that a ruling from Strasbourg would minimise the possible subsequent use of the so-called interrogation techniques, not only by the UK but by any government anywhere in the world.

The Strasbourg case required detailed work in Northern Ireland by the Department of Foreign Affairs in support of the attorney general and his impressive legal team. When Eamonn Gallagher was transferred to the EEC division in 1972 my role was expanded, and though I was never given a new job description, I assumed that my job was to monitor and assess what was happening generally in Northern Ireland with an emphasis on the political situation. My colleague Michael Lillis took over the Strasbourg case, including organising the hooded men and other witnesses to travel to hearings in Strasbourg and at a remote military base in Norway, when the UK refused to allow its military witnesses to appear in Strasbourg.

ANGLO-IRISH RELATIONS IN THE 1970s

There were good times and there were bad times. The Sunningdale Conference in December 1973 was a particularly high point. In his impressive account, *Sunningdale: the search for peace in Northern Ireland* (Dublin, 2017), Noel Dorr argues that it marked a historic turning point in Anglo-Irish attempts to deal with Northern Ireland. It was important not only in its recognition of Dublin's role; it also effectively provided a map for subsequent settlement efforts including the Good Friday Agreement.

There were also many low points in the years 1974–84 before we returned to a positive phase that led to the Anglo-Irish Agreement in 1985. These included the behaviour of the security forces in Northern Ireland, which was a constant source of disagreement between Dublin and London. Not only did it give rise to problems for the nationalist community; it complicated the development of north–south security cooperation that was so vital for both parts of Ireland. The concentration by some secretaries of state for Northern Ireland, notably Roy Mason, on security policies to the virtual exclusion of political initiatives suggested that London had learned nothing from failed security policies such as the introduction of internment and from Bloody Sunday, both of which had resulted in increased support for the Provisional IRA.

Another constant irritant in Anglo-Irish relations was the difference in approaches to the Provisional IRA. The Irish government, recognising that the IRA's objectives included the overthrow by force of the government in Dublin, had a strict policy of no contact whatsoever with any organisation engaged in or supporting violence. In contrast, the UK authorities had, from the very early days following the introduction of direct rule, maintained either direct or indirect contact with the leadership of the Provisional IRA. This began on 20 June 1972 when two senior British officials, Philip Woodfield and Frank Steele, met Gerry Adams and Dáithí Ó Conaill in a house in Donegal. Care had been taken on both sides to establish the validity of the other's credentials. There was no room to doubt Adams's role as a leader of the Provisional IRA. A larger meeting followed in London in July that year, and there is little doubt that contact was maintained in subsequent years, even in the midst of the most appalling atrocities committed by the Provisionals. The constant denial by the British of any contact tended to create an atmosphere of mistrust at the highest level in Dublin and inhibited the development of normal intergovernmental relationships.

There was a particularly difficult episode in 1974 after the collapse of the Sunningdale arrangements. Harold Wilson had become prime minister following the February elections, and shortly after assuming office he directed that the option of unilateral British withdrawal from Northern Ireland should be examined. It seemed likely that the British had alerted the Provisional IRA to this. The Irish government had not been informed at any level, and whatever information we had came from London-based journalists who were known to be close to the Labour Party. The proposition was considered at a number of sessions of a Cabinet committee on Northern Ireland, and attracted, surprisingly, the support of some ministers, including Roy Jenkins. Disagreements within the Cabinet and strong negative advice from civil servants, notably Robert Armstrong, finally saw the proposition dropped, but not before relations with Harold Wilson hit rock bottom. He was never trusted by Dublin again.

One plus in the 1970s was that the Irish government now had a good network of Northern Ireland contacts maintained by officials from the Department of Foreign Affairs. I spent much time in Northern Ireland through the decade and developed close relationships with many of the leading political figures, mainly on the nationalist side. My pattern of work was to call on politicians for a chat, sometimes over a meal, and summarise the conversations in reports that were normally circulated to the minister, the taoiseach and relevant officials. I became particularly close to the SDLP and attended many of their conferences and think-ins. As July and August were times of particular tension, many Northerners, including politicians, rented holiday homes in Donegal; I did likewise and moved with my family every July to Bunbeg, where the

Humes were long-time summer residents. From 1974 on, contact with unionists was maintained by my colleague John McColgan.

In 1969 the UK government had responded to its need for accurate information about Northern Ireland by establishing a presence in Laneside, a house in a quiet laneway off the Belfast to Bangor Road, not far from Holywood. It tended to be staffed by officials with a security/intelligence background, who were unable for personal safety reasons to travel freely around Northern Ireland. They did, however, build up a good network of contacts from all sections of the community, no doubt including groups engaged in violence. I was an occasional visitor there myself, trading selected information in the way in which diplomats traditionally do.

Officially the UK did not welcome those of us from the Department of Foreign Affairs who travelled on business in Northern Ireland. The British ambassador in Dublin approached my minister and the taoiseach a number of times objecting to what I was doing, and making it clear that they could not guarantee my safety. I now know from Laneside papers recently released and declassified that I was deemed to be the 'head of Irish Intelligence in Northern Ireland'. Given the circulation of papers between the multiplicity of UK security agencies, including the Royal Ulster Constabulary (RUC), the British army, British intelligence services (MI5, MI6) and the Ulster Defence Regiment (UDR), and the collusion that has been established between these agencies and loyalist paramilitary organisations, I am relieved that I survived unscathed for seven years. The department had given me absolutely no advice on personal safety, but equally had placed no restrictions on what I did or how I did it.

On one occasion what I was doing was recognised in an unusual, possibly unique way. During the 1974 Ulster Workers' Council (UWC) strike that brought down the Sunningdale arrangements, I travelled every day between Dublin and Belfast, mainly to maintain contact with the SDLP and other members of the fledgling Northern Ireland executive. Roads were blocked, petrol was unobtainable, electricity was cut off in many areas, loyalists paramilitaries were in charge and there was a general air of chaos. When it was all over, the taoiseach, Liam Cosgrave, sent for me and in the presence of my minister thanked me for my services and handed me an envelope. It contained £500 in notes. I subsequently discovered that the money came from the Secret Service fund.

US INVOLVEMENT

Official US policy since 1922 was not to get involved in the Northern Ireland issue. The Americans slavishly followed the British line. Even the presidency of John F. Kennedy accepted that the special relationship with London required that nothing be said or done that might upset the status quo. There was no reference to Northern Ireland in any of the speeches made by Kennedy during his 1963 visit to Ireland.

The turnaround, beginning with President Carter, was all the more remarkable coming as it did from one of the few US presidents for whom we were unable to find an Irish connection. It happened because of four American-Irish politicians who held key positions (and who became known as the Four Horsemen), combined with the persistent lobbying by John Hume and the skills and energy of Michael Lillis, then a counsellor in the Irish embassy in Washington.

From the beginning of the Troubles there was concern in Dublin at the flow of funds and arms from the US to the Provisional IRA. Politicians such as Speaker Tip O'Neill, Senators Kennedy and Moynihan and Governor Hugh Carey of New York were recruited in the efforts to reduce this support. In conversations with John Hume they came to the view that their approach would be more effective if they had a positive as well as a negative message to impart. President Carter had assumed office in 1977, and as a newcomer to Washington politics he quickly recognised the importance of good relations with older Washington hands, especially fellow Democrats who held key positions. O'Neill as speaker of the House of Representatives was particularly important as an ally who would facilitate the passage of Carter's legislative proposals.

Working closely with John Hume and Michael Lillis, the Four Horsemen developed the idea of having the president issue a statement on St Patrick's Day, 1977. Opposition from the State Department and the British embassy delayed the statement but President Carter issued it in August 1977; it was another turning point in the approach to the Northern Ireland problem. It recognised that any solution must involve both parts of the community in Northern Ireland as well as the British and Irish governments. Additionally, at John Hume's request, it included a commitment that in the event of a settlement, the US government would be prepared to join with others to see how additional job-creating investment in Northern Ireland could be encouraged. The primary significance of the statement, however, was that for the first time a US government acknowledged a role in Northern Ireland for an Irish government. Subsequently Carter said that the State Department 'was not in favour of what I did … But I didn't really consult them too thoroughly. I had a lot of confidence in Pat Moynihan, and Tip O'Neill was visiting me every day. Hugh Carey was very important to me as a politician, so was Ted Kennedy.'

The challenge was to maintain and develop US interest when Carter was succeeded by Ronald Reagan in 1981. Fortunately, Reagan had an interest in Ireland. He had visited in the 1950s and loved to recount his staying in the Gresham Hotel in Dublin and watching young people dancing at a stylish white-tie ball. He noted with particular interest that some of the couples went home on bikes, the male tucking his trousers into his socks and the female tucking her long gown somewhere so that she could sit on the crossbar. When I asked him about his Irish roots he said he didn't think he had any, but he did arrange to send me some family papers and through various genealogical sources it was established that the family had partly originated in Ballyporeen in County Tipperary. He agreed to come to the Irish embassy for a celebratory lunch on his first St Patrick's Day as president, at which he was presented with an illustrated family tree. It was at that lunch that Speaker O'Neill arranged for the president to attend a lunch on Capitol Hill the following St Patrick's Day —an arrangement that has been honoured by every president and every speaker since. Reagan continued to show an interest in Ireland and made a state visit, including to Ballyporeen, in 1984.

On the policy side Reagan entrusted Irish affairs to Bill Clark, one of his inner circle who was successively deputy secretary of state and national security adviser. I kept Clark fully briefed on Anglo-Irish relations and specifically on the negotiation of the

Anglo-Irish Agreement. When the negotiations stalled following Thatcher's 'out, out, out' comments, Reagan, briefed by Clark and encouraged by O'Neill, raised the matter with Thatcher and the negotiations were put back on the rails. When the agreement was signed, Reagan and O'Neill gave a joint press conference at the White House in which they backed the agreement and announced that they would honour Carter's 1977 promise.

The US involvement continued, and President Clinton's role in making possible the Good Friday Agreement is well known and is covered elsewhere in this book. The appointment of Senator George Mitchell as special representative for Northern Ireland was especially inspiring.

CONCLUSION

The changes brought about by politicians and diplomats in the 1970s and 1980s were a huge help in making possible the Good Friday Agreement. The commitment of successive taoisigh and British prime ministers, the courage and vision of Northern Ireland politicians, the active interest of leading US politicians and the professionalism of a generation of civil servants and diplomats combined to make it all happen.

The Years Before Good Friday: Some Personal Memories

NOEL DORR

I first became actively involved in issues relating to Northern Ireland in 1969 while I was a first secretary in the Irish embassy in Washington—though still only for a short time and to a limited degree.

In August I was home on leave in the west of Ireland. Following serious trouble in Belfast and Derry after the Apprentice Boys' march, the government sent Minister for External Affairs Patrick Hillery to New York to ask the UN Security Council for a peacekeeping force for Northern Ireland. I was called back to Dublin for a few days and helped my colleagues in the UN section prepare a memorandum for the government on this issue.

My first substantial involvement in Northern Ireland issues came a year later when I was transferred home and assigned to the press and information section. There I dealt with journalists from around the world who came in increasing numbers to report on the growing conflict in Northern Ireland. I also dealt regularly with the resident Irish correspondents of three important British news media—*The Times,* the *Financial Times* and the BBC.

Many of the visiting journalists and columnists were British. Others were the London correspondents of European and American news media. In London they had ready access to the UK government view. They now wanted to spend a few days on the ground in Northern Ireland to cover the story and they also wanted a view from Dublin. My job was to ensure that they were facilitated and briefed on Irish government policy. As well as talking to them initially myself, I usually set up an appointment or a lunch with an official in the department such as Eamon Gallagher, who, for a time, played an important role as adviser and speech-writer to the taoiseach, Jack Lynch. Sometimes we arranged a meeting, or perhaps a discussion over lunch, with the taoiseach or with some other government minister. In the early years it was not always easy to ensure a meeting with an authoritative spokesperson at political level—but things improved greatly over time. Jack Lynch in particular created a good impression. I would also arrange for them to meet opposition spokespersons, academics and others in public life to give them a broader view of opinion here. On occasion, we arranged a group visit for journalists such as the Westminster lobby correspondents. After briefing in Dublin and, perhaps, lunch with the taoiseach or another minister, we took them for a few days on a visit to some scenic area in Ireland.

During those years, the British government continually pressed the Irish government to improve cross-border security cooperation. Jack Lynch responded that the centre of the problem was in Northern Ireland—particularly the 'no-go areas' just across the border. He was clear in rejecting violence but he continued to maintain Irish unity, achieved by peaceful means only, as our long-term aim. He pressed Prime Minister Ted Heath on two points—the unsuitability of devolution based on majority rule in the divided society of Northern Ireland and the need to accept the role of the Irish government in achieving a settlement.

In May 1972 I was promoted to counsellor and undertook overall responsibility for the department's press and information section. Shortly before this, a new 'Anglo-Irish division' had been set up to deal with British–Irish relations and Northern Ireland issues, in cooperation with the taoiseach's department and the Department of Justice. Its head was Bob McDonagh, an assistant secretary. Eamonn Gallagher, a counsellor, worked under him, but Eamonn also had an unusual measure of direct contact with the taoiseach during his time as adviser and speech-writer on Northern Ireland.

The most important part of our work in the information section related to Northern Ireland issues, so our section became part of the new Anglo-Irish division. As a result, I was drawn into drafting occasional speeches and articles for the taoiseach—for example, a long article on the Northern Ireland problem he contributed to the US journal *Foreign Affairs* in 1972—and contributing to policy issues relating to Northern Ireland, where primary responsibility rested with my colleagues in the main section of the Northern Ireland division: Eamonn Gallagher, Seán Donlon, John Swift and Joe Small.

1972 was one of the worst years of the Troubles. Bloody Sunday in Derry was followed by the burning of the British embassy in Dublin. In March the British government imposed direct rule from London and began to look for some better basis for restoring devolution. In October the secretary of state for Northern Ireland, Willie Whitelaw, published a discussion document—a green paper. It was welcomed by the Irish government because in important respects, it reflected ideas Jack Lynch had been pressing on Heath over the previous eighteen months. It envisaged a devolved administration with a sharing of power between Northern Ireland parties; and it recognised, for the first time, that the 'Irish dimension' intrinsic to Northern Ireland had to be given expression in seeking to settle the conflict there.

Contacts and exchanges between the two governments now became more frequent and more positive, directed as they were to building on the ideas of the green paper; and there was less of the occasional recrimination of the early years of the Troubles. It helped that both countries, having signed accession treaties in January 1972, became EEC members on 1 January 1973.

The Government of Ireland Act 1920, which created Northern Ireland, provided for a Council of Ireland, though it never came into existence. There was now renewed interest in the idea as a way of giving institutional expression to 'the Irish dimension'—even on the part of Ulster Unionist Party (UUP) leader Brian Faulkner, who saw it primarily as a way to promote greater cross-border security cooperation. Irish government policy—under Jack Lynch up to early 1973, and the coalition government led by Taoiseach Liam Cosgrave and Tánaiste Brendan Corish from March 1973—focused on achieving new political institutions: a power-sharing devolved administration in Northern Ireland, and—to give expression to 'the Irish dimension'—a strong north–south Council of Ireland with executive functions as well as a consultative role and a capacity to develop, by agreement, over time.

In March 1973, the British government published a white paper on Northern Ireland. It envisaged a conference, involving the two governments and elected parties from Northern Ireland, later that year. Over the following nine months there were regular and intensive meetings and exchanges of position papers and proposals at official level between the two governments. In September, Heath and Liam Cosgrave had a day-long meeting at Casement aerodrome in Baldonnel, Dublin. Along with other officials on the Irish side, I was deeply involved in this work, in addition to my role in dealing with the press on Northern Ireland issues; and I was part of the taoiseach's delegation for the Baldonnel meeting.

Following the election of a new Northern Ireland Assembly in June 1973, and intensive talks chaired by Willie Whitelaw, the leaders of the three assembly parties willing to participate—Ulster Unionists, SDLP and Alliance—agreed in November 1973 to form a power-sharing executive. This, and the intensive exchanges between the two governments on the role and structures of a Council of Ireland, cleared the way for a conference at Sunningdale in early December.

The agreed communiqué provided for a north–south Council of Ireland with an executive and a consultative role, as well as various measures that could help improve security cooperation. A second session of the conference was to be held some months later, when the executive functions of the Council had been worked out. A formal agreement would then be signed and registered at the United Nations. I was part of the Irish delegation at Sunningdale and played a part in drafting the opening and closing statements of the taoiseach.

The agreement cleared the way for the power-sharing Northern Ireland executive to take office on 1 January 1974. But support in the unionist party and community for what Brian Faulkner had agreed at Sunningdale proved weak. It diminished further over the following months and the second conference never took place. As unionist and loyalist opposition grew, Faulkner became steadily weaker. Finally, a strike of loyalist electricity workers in May that threatened to paralyse Northern Ireland led to the collapse of the executive and, in practice, the end of Sunningdale.

In May 1974 I became head of the political division. Over the next six years, first as assistant secretary and then as deputy secretary, I dealt largely with foreign policy cooperation between EEC member states and had no direct role in relation to Northern Ireland issues. In May 1980, however, I was involved in the preparations for the first meeting between the taoiseach, Charles Haughey, and the British prime minister, Margaret Thatcher, and I was part of the official delegation that accompanied him at the meeting. In September 1980 I was appointed permanent representative to the UN and so I was not at their second meeting in Dublin Castle in December. Those meetings led to a new emphasis on 'the totality of relations' between Britain and Ireland as a context within which to address the Northern Ireland conflict. However, the long-term possibilities inherent in this approach were oversold on our side. This, together with the position taken by the taoiseach as the Falklands war developed in May 1982, and bitterness left by the British handling of Northern Ireland hunger strikes, greatly soured the developing relationship with Mrs Thatcher.

During my three years at the UN, which included our two-year term on the Security Council in 1981–82, I had no role on Northern Ireland matters. However, on several occasions I was called home to participate in small informal 'think-ins' on the issue organised by the then taoiseach, Garret FitzGerald. In August 1983 I moved to London as ambassador to the UK.

At the time the taoiseach was deeply concerned about the deteriorating situation in Northern Ireland and deep bitterness and alienation in the minority community. He greatly feared that with increased electoral support, Sinn Féin, a party linked closely with the IRA, might displace the SDLP, who were committed to a non-violent, political approach, and then present itself in the US as 'the voice of the minority'. The need for a new approach to try to achieve a Northern Ireland settlement seemed obvious. But the outlook was not promising. Mrs Thatcher had lost a close adviser, Airey Neave, to an Irish National Liberation Army (INLA) bomb; her relationship with the previous taoiseach had soured, and her general attitude to Northern Ireland might be summarised as 'better leave bad enough alone'. Nevertheless, Garret FitzGerald set himself to persuade her to work towards a new initiative.

In an informal discussion with British Deputy Cabinet Secretary David Goodall in September 1983, Michael Lillis, head of the Anglo-Irish division, with prior authorisation from the taoiseach, outlined ideas he described as strictly personal. They envisaged an 'imaginative transformation' in Northern Ireland, achieved by the direct involvement on the ground in Northern Ireland of Irish security forces and courts with which the minority community could identify. This, in effect, pointed towards something approaching 'joint authority' between the two governments—balanced, to meet unionist fears, by a willingness of the Irish government to review the 'claim' to Northern Ireland in articles 2 and 3 of the constitution.

Garret FitzGerald explored these ideas further at a summit at Chequers with Margaret Thatcher in November 1983. Her initial response was none too promising, but in early 1984—influenced by Foreign Secretary Geoffrey Howe and officials such as Cabinet Secretary Sir Robert Armstrong and David Goodall —she authorised further contacts at official level. This led to intensive confidential negotiations over nearly two years, conducted in the first instance by two small teams of officials led by the respective cabinet secretaries—Robert Armstrong and Dermot Nally—under the authority of the prime minister and the taoiseach. The negotiations were intensified after publication of the New Ireland Forum report in May 1984. They involved regular meetings, in most cases over two days, on one side or other of the Irish Sea, between the two teams of officials—up to 36 such meetings in all. At ministerial level, the ministers for foreign affairs and justice met from time to time with the British foreign and Northern Ireland secretaries. The two heads of government, Garret FitzGerald and Margaret Thatcher, followed the negotiations closely and gave instructions to their respective negotiators at each stage. They held summit meetings at Chequers in 1983 and 1984 and also met from time to time on the margins of European Council meetings.

The outcome was the Anglo-Irish Agreement signed by both heads of government at Hillsborough on 15 November 1985 and subsequently registered at the United Nations as an international treaty. The agreement was unprecedented and proved to be of long-term importance. It established political structures—an Anglo-Irish intergovernmental conference and a joint secretariat in Belfast—through which, for the first time, the Irish government was entitled to offer views and proposals in regard to direct rule in Northern Ireland. Both governments were committed to 'determined' efforts to reach agreement.

As ambassador in London from 1983 to 1987 I attended all these meetings at ministerial and summit level. In meeting and entertaining British ministers, other Westminster politicians and senior officials, and in frequent speaking engagements, I also did what I could to explain Irish government policies and to build support in London at ministerial, political and official levels for our approach. My colleague in the embassy Richard Ryan took on the particular task of working on backbencher MPs in the Conservative Party to build support for a positive approach by the prime minister to resolving the Northern Ireland issue.

I was deeply involved in the 'Armstrong–Nally' talks, which I was instructed, for much of the time, to keep absolutely confidential—even within the embassy—and after each meeting I reported in detail on our discussions. I also reported regularly on the views of British ministers, politicians and senior officials on whom I called, or met socially, or entertained in the embassy. Both governments were exploring the possibility of an initiative, with no certainty about the outcome, and each was trying to measure what it should offer and what the other side might accept. I think our reports were read closely in Dublin, not least by the taoiseach who followed the negotiations closely.

In March 1987, just as the Fine Gael–Labour coalition government left office and Fianna Fáil came back to power, I was appointed secretary (the post is now secretary general) of the Department of Foreign Affairs, in succession to Seán Donlon.

The Anglo-Irish Agreement was nearly a year and a half in place. There had been regular meetings of the Anglo-Irish intergovernmental conference at ministerial level; the joint Anglo-Irish secretariat in Belfast, headed on the Irish side by Michael Lillis, a principal architect of the agreement, had weathered the extreme difficulties caused by unionist and loyalist outrage and was working the agreement to the full on a day-to-day basis. The incoming taoiseach, Charles Haughey, however, had publicly opposed the agreement while in opposition and sent Brian Lenihan, now appointed Minister for Foreign Affairs, to Washington to lobby against it. So there was a question as to what attitude he would take as taoiseach.

In the event he explicitly accepted the Anglo-Irish Agreement as a commitment of the state that his government would uphold. Brian Lenihan and Minister for Justice Gerard Collins regularly attended the Anglo-Irish Intergovernmental Conference, where Lenihan developed a good working and personal relationship with the Northern secretary, Tom King.

As taoiseach, Charles Haughey took an active, directive role in the operation of the agreement on the Irish side, and, indeed, on most areas of government. Furthermore, for nearly a year while Brian Lenihan underwent serious medical treatment abroad, the taoiseach assumed direct responsibility for our department. So I dealt directly with him, not just as taoiseach but as our minister. Granted the understandable tendency of any incoming government to wonder about the role of the civil service that had worked well with its predecessors, I was concerned to establish that we in the Department of Foreign Affairs would work professionally, with integrity and political impartiality, for whatever government was democratically elected by the people.

Margaret Thatcher deserves credit for signing the agreement and standing by it in the face of vehement unionist opposition. But she had become very critical of what she saw as the less than whole-hearted cross-border security cooperation by the Irish government, which she expected to be one of the agreement's greatest benefits. Although later, in her memoirs, she speaks quite positively of Charles Haughey, there must have been a strong residual memory on her side, and indeed also on his, of tensions between them in the early 1980s. So there were frequent episodes of difficulty and recrimination in their relationship over Northern Ireland during this period.

Dermot Gallagher, head of the Anglo-Irish division, and Sean O hUiginn, who succeeded Michael Lillis in the secretariat in Belfast, both worked assiduously on Northern Ireland issues in those years. However, as former ambassador in London and, now, as secretary of the department working directly to the taoiseach, I felt a particular responsibility for helping to smooth such difficulties as arose in working the agreement and in the Anglo-Irish relationship. I remember particularly working well professionally over this period with the British ambassador, Sir Nicholas Fenn, as we both did what we could to ensure that Anglo-Irish cooperation over Northern Ireland would weather episodes of exasperation or recrimination on one or other side of the Irish Sea. Indeed, I had the impression that he was sometimes criticised—even berated—by his prime minister for appearing too understanding in explaining Irish government policies to her.

A great merit of the Anglo-Irish Agreement was that tensions and difficulties that arose at times between Dublin and London were now handled within established structures. True, the agreement did not resolve the conflict in Northern Ireland: though welcomed by the SDLP it was opposed by Sinn Féin and the republican movement; and vehemently and forcefully rejected by unionists and loyalists. Nevertheless, though neither side would openly acknowledge this, I would argue that, over time and in different ways, it helped bring movement to hitherto intransigent parties on both sides of the community divide, and thereby helped prepare the way for developments in the 1990s that led eventually to the Belfast/Good Friday Agreement of 1998.

On the one hand the leadership of Sinn Féin and the republican movement—already, perhaps, privately beginning to rethink their approach—came gradually, through discussions with John Hume and others, to see what could be achieved through political means. This led to various back-channel contacts and soundings by each of the two governments that extended in due course also to loyalists, and eventually led to the ceasefires of the 1990s and the subsequent involvement of Sinn Féin in the talks leading to the 1998 agreement. On the other hand, unionist dislike of the Anglo-Irish Agreement was so great that when they were unable to pull it down, they became more open, over time, to negotiations that might lead to some alternative.

This opened the way for the Stormont or 'Brooke–Mayhew' talks of the early 1990s, in which I was actively involved.

The basis was a statement by Northern Ireland Secretary Peter Brooke in the House of Commons in November 1990. The four main constitutional parties in Northern Ireland—Ulster Unionists, Democratic Unionist Party (DUP), SDLP and Alliance—and the two governments were now, he said, prepared to work for 'a new beginning for relationships within Northern Ireland, within the island of Ireland and between the peoples of these islands'. The talks were in three strands, corresponding to the three interlocking relationships. The unionist parties, initially, wanted the Anglo-Irish Agreement suspended for the duration of the talks. They were induced to participate when the governments agreed to defer meetings of the ministerial Anglo-Irish intergovernmental conference while talks were under way. The secretariat would not need to service the conference during that period, though its other work would continue.

Strand 1, confined to the four Northern Ireland parties and chaired by Brooke's successor, Sir Patrick Mayhew, began on 29 April 1992. Strand 2, involving the two governments as well as the four parties, opened in London on 6 July under the chairmanship of Sir Ninian Stephen, former governor-general of Australia. Strand 2 continued in Stormont, and on one occasion in Dublin, over the following months, until late November. The two governments also met on occasion as Strand 3. I was deeply involved in these talks over about six months, along with colleagues including secretaries of the Justice and Defence departments Joe Brosnan and Sean Brosnan, and Sean O hUiginn, head of the Anglo-Irish division in Foreign Affairs, accompanying ministers at meetings and occasionally attending a procedural committee. The Irish government was represented by four ministers: Tánaiste John Wilson (Defence), David Andrews (Foreign Affairs), Padraig Flynn (Justice) and Des O'Malley (Industry and Commerce) (occasionally replaced by Mary Harney).

The 'Brooke–Mayhew talks' are little remembered now. It was too much to hope that in themselves they could lead to a Northern Ireland settlement. There were already indirect contacts by both governments, through intermediaries, with extreme elements on both sides in the hope of persuading them to a ceasefire. This led in due course to the painstaking negotiation of texts that became the basis for the negotiations leading to the Good Friday/Belfast Agreement of 1998.

Nevertheless, notwithstanding their disappointing outcome at the time, and the fact that extreme elements, still engaged in violence, were not yet represented at the table, 'the Stormont talks' helped to put some pieces in place for that later, more comprehensive negotiation. For the first time since partition, Irish government ministers sat opposite unionist party leaders—including, remarkably, Ian Paisley and the DUP—as well as the leaders of the SDLP and Alliance, for a discussion of future relations on the island. Every other negotiation or discussion since 1920—with the partial exceptions, perhaps, of 1925 and Sunningdale—was primarily with the British government. The British were also present at these talks, but—following Peter Brooke's statement on 9 November 1990 that they had 'no selfish strategic or economic interest in Northern Ireland'—they professed to be ready to accept virtually any outcome the other participants could agree on. So, in effect, the real future negotiation would be between unionism and nationalism in Ireland. Months of argument also had an educational effect on all sides in clarifying issues and conditioning participants for the more comprehensive negotiation that lay ahead. Unionists began to accept, tacitly at least, that the hated Anglo-Irish Agreement could be superseded only by a more comprehensive agreement providing for power-sharing and an 'Irish dimension' involving the Irish government; and Northern nationalists and the Irish government could see that for such an agreement, articles 2 and 3 would have to be on the table.

In the meantime, still well below the horizon, contacts with more extreme elements through intermediaries were beginning to be discussed, cautiously and confidentially, between the two governments. I recall going to London in early 1992 with Dermot Nally and Sean O hUiginn to explore on behalf of the taoiseach, with Sir Robin Butler, the Cabinet secretary and John Chilcot of the Northern Ireland Office, the scope for such contacts by the two governments. They showed some cautious interest in the possibility but not until after the forthcoming election. Later, as back-channel contacts with Sinn Féin and loyalists developed, and the two governments exchanged documents, I had a somewhat peripheral role in work being done mainly by Martin Mansergh, Sean O hUiginn and Fergus Finlay. I was with the taoiseach, Albert Reynolds, in Downing Street when he and John Major issued the seminal Downing Street Declaration on 15 December 1993 and with the taoiseach, John Bruton, for the Framework Document in February 1995.

By then I had served for eight years as secretary. I decided I ought to retire, some years earlier than the normal retirement date. I did so on 30 June 1995, three years before the Good Friday Agreement settlement of an issue in which, as an official, I had played a part, with many others, over 25 years.

The New Ireland Forum: Redefining Irish Nationalism and Setting the Agenda for the Anglo-Irish Agreement

TED SMYTH

When I joined the Department of Foreign Affairs in late 1972, it was focused on managing two major political initiatives: the republic's imminent accession to the EEC and the escalating Northern Ireland conflict, including preparations to take the UK government to the European Court of Human Rights and negotiations for what would become the Sunningdale Conference the following year. My assignment in 1973 to the newly formed European Political Cooperation unit included support for the first European summit in Dublin Castle (Foreign Minister Garret FitzGerald committed Irish officials to conduct meetings through French rather than English), which led to a year in Geneva as a delegate to the East–West Commission on Security and Cooperation in Europe (CSCE) talks. Next came a posting to the Irish embassy in Portugal during the revolution that ousted the fascist government. Henry Kissinger wrongly concluded that Portugal was lost to communism, but European support for Mário Soares's Socialist party resulted in him defeating the communists in the first free elections in Portugal.

While in Portugal I got to know scores of senior journalists who covered the revolution, including Mike Burns and Liam Hourican from RTÉ, Paul Gillespie from *The Irish Times* and Robert Fisk, then with *The Times*. The deteriorating situation in Northern Ireland was never far from our minds, and I thus welcomed an offer in 1976 from Seán Donlon, then assistant secretary of the Anglo-Irish division, to become head of press in the United States. Working with brilliant diplomatic colleagues over the next four years, including Michael Lillis, Seán Donlon (who became ambassador to the US in 1978), Gearóid Ó Cléirigh, Padraic Collins, Sean O hUiginn and Jim Sharkey, five basic goals were pursued: secure American political and public support for a Northern Ireland solution based on a role for Dublin and equal rights for nationalists and unionists, encourage Irish-Americans to support this objective rather than IRA violence, persuade the traditionally pro-British American media to become more critical of the British government's one-sided policy in Northern Ireland, work with the Industrial Development Authority (IDA) to attract foreign direct investment to Ireland and, finally, collaborate with Irish-Americans to promote Irish culture and the arts.

Availing of the visits of Irish politicians, especially John Hume, we made progress on a number of these goals. As Seán Donlon has noted in this volume, Michael Lillis (who had preceded me as Head of Press) worked with the Four Horsemen to convince President Carter in 1977 to break with precedent and support a Dublin role in Northern Ireland. We eventually secured widespread media support for this historic breakthrough despite Jody Powell's (Carter's press secretary) best efforts to bury the announcement on a Friday evening in August; doubtless an effort to placate an angry State Department and British government.

However, much of the progress by Irish politicians and diplomats in advocating a peaceful solution was endangered by the intransigence of British Prime Minister Margaret Thatcher in relation to the IRA hunger strikes begun in 1980. IRA prisoners in Northern Ireland went on hunger strike to restore the right to wear their own clothes as political prisoners. These protests escalated dramatically in 1981, resulting in the election of Bobby Sands to the British parliament during his hunger strike. Sands died in May

1981 following the British government's refusal to make concessions on prison rules, despite appeals for flexibility from Taoiseach Charles Haughey and the Four Horsemen. Ten hunger strikers died in all before the strike was called off amid an escalation of sectarian violence in Northern Ireland and a surge of sympathy for the dead republicans among Irish nationalists and Irish America. In elections in Northern Ireland between 1983 and 1984 Sinn Féin averaged 12 per cent of the total vote and 40 per cent of the nationalist vote. Faced with the growing alienation of nationalists in Northern Ireland and British inaction, John Hume and the SDLP concluded that constitutional nationalists needed to develop new policies for Northern Ireland that would provide a path to peace between the two communities.

In his memoirs Garret FitzGerald recalled that when he succeeded Charles Haughey as taoiseach in December 1982, Hume proposed a Council for a New Ireland that would bring together constitutional non-violent nationalist parties in Ireland, but FitzGerald, who wanted to include unionists, thought the term 'Council' 'would remind Unionists too forcibly of the "Council of Ireland" proposal in the Sunningdale Agreement'. FitzGerald hoped to secure a two-fold result: 'a set of principles for the achievement of peace and stability in Northern Ireland' and the emergence of a number of models, including acceptance of a joint sovereignty or joint authority model that would 'have eliminated, or at any rate greatly weakened, a possible Fianna Fáil objection to whatever might ultimately emerge from a negotiation, which would inevitably be something other than a united Ireland'. In 1980 when he was taoiseach, Haughey had held a meeting with Prime Minister Thatcher at which, in a secret memo, 'a joint defence pact was offered in return for political movement'. Thatcher was furious when Irish ministers then claimed a united Ireland would be possible within ten years. Relations deteriorated further during the IRA hunger strikes and the Falklands war of 1982.

Hume's immediate goal was to create an alternative forum to the Northern Ireland Assembly, which the SDLP had boycotted because it lacked an all-Ireland dimension, but he also wished to develop new political initiatives for peace, which had been virtually non-existent since the collapse of Sunningdale in 1974. Hume,

FitzGerald and Tánaiste Dick Spring were united in the belief that some type of non-boycottable British–Irish intergovernmental structure would be needed to govern Northern Ireland, given that loyalist and IRA paramilitaries had the ability to destroy internal power-sharing institutions such as those agreed at Sunningdale.

FitzGerald later recalled that when he initially presented the Forum proposal to his Cabinet (a coalition of Fine Gael and Labour), it was opposed by twelve votes to two because of fears that the Forum would distract the newly formed government from 'exceptionally pressing domestic problems'. (The Cabinet's concerns were understandable given that a previous FitzGerald government had, a year earlier, been defeated over budget proposals.) He subsequently succeeded in securing his Cabinet's support using the political argument that Haughey as leader of the opposition had indicated he would support Hume's proposal, putting the government in the embarrassing position of appearing to be ignoring the plight of the north. The political risks involved in convening the Forum were undeniably high. There was always the possibility that the parties would be unable to reach agreement, seriously weakening constitutional nationalism. Moreover, FitzGerald and Spring would be committing to a partnership on Northern Ireland with Haughey, potentially limiting their options in government. Notably, in the 1950s, Éamon de Valera as taoiseach had resisted efforts by Northern Ireland nationalists for an all-Ireland consultative body.

On 11 March 1983 the Irish government announced the formation of an all-island forum for 'consultations on the manner in which lasting peace and stability can be achieved in a new Ireland through the democratic process'. Participation would be 'open to all democratic parties which reject violence, and which have members elected or appointed to the Oireachtas or the Northern Ireland Assembly'. FitzGerald cleared the announcement with Tánaiste Dick Spring, Haughey and Hume. *Boston Globe* journalist Steve Erlanger wrote in April that this initiative would be a bold and risky attempt by constitutional nationalists to head off 'a possibly disastrous radicalization of Northern nationalist opinion' as 'British officials admit that Britain finds itself without an effective policy in Northern Ireland and in need of one.'

All the unionist parties and the Alliance Party declined to participate formally in the forum, but their representatives sent written submissions, and some presented at plenary sessions in Dublin Castle. Thus, the New Ireland Forum, with four participating parties—Fianna Fáil, Fine Gael, the Labour Party and the SDLP—representing 80 per cent of the island's population (and over 90 per cent of Irish nationalists), became the first all-island platform for Irish nationalism since 1920. Many observers were sceptical of the exercise; in addition to unionist detractors, there were some in the south who feared that the forum would be a one-sided pan-nationalist body designed to attack the British and unionism. Conor Cruise O'Brien called it the 'make-believe' forum and advised John Hume to stay at home. The leader of the Workers' Party, Tomás Mac Giolla, rejected FitzGerald's invitation, asserting that the forum's primary aim was to 'bail out the SDLP' and the 'net effect of your efforts to date has been to close the ranks of Unionism and consolidate them behind their age-old slogans and attitudes' (as quoted by Frank Sheridan). Thatcher thought the forum 'complicated things' and was not impressed by Dublin's argument that it would buttress John Hume's position within his community, which was being subverted by Sinn Féin (quoted in Paul Routledge's biography of Hume). However, the Congressional Friends of Ireland in Washington passed a resolution on 17 March declaring that a real solution would require 'the bold cooperation of the British and Irish governments jointly pursuing, at the highest levels, a new strategy of reconciliation'.

In early May 1983 Thatcher herself 'complicated things' for Northern Ireland by calling a general election that resulted in the SDLP securing 17.9 per cent and Sinn Féin 13.4 per cent of the vote, an alarmingly high endorsement of IRA violence. While John Hume won a seat in Foyle/Derry, Sinn Féin leader Gerry Adams won in West Belfast, with unionists winning the remaining 15 seats. SDLP members Seamus Mallon and Eddie McGrady narrowly missed winning seats. Thatcher meanwhile capitalised on her victory in the Falkland Islands, securing a Conservative Party majority of 144, the largest majority since the Labour landslide of 1945.

Notwithstanding political rivalries, the four party leaders took their duties regarding the forum very seriously from the beginning, holding the first of 56 meetings of their steering group on 14 April 1983. They agreed that they would determine the agenda, the programme of work and deadlines, and then oversee the preparation of the final report. They appointed their most senior and experienced representatives to the forum, with 27 members and 14 alternate members, many of them ministers or former ministers, including Minister for Foreign Affairs Peter Barry, Enda Kenny, Maurice Manning, Brian Lenihan, Ray McSharry, Gerry Collins, Frank Cluskey, Mary Robinson, Seamus Mallon, Austin Currie, Joe Hendron, Eddie McGrady and Hugh Logue. Each party employed a secretary to engage with its members and the secretariat (members and secretariat are listed in the appendix). The Fianna Fáil secretary was Veronica Guerin, who became a renowned *Sunday Independent* reporter, later to be brutally murdered by a drug criminal.

The selection of an independent chair for the forum tested relations among the party leaders at the outset, with Haughey vetoing FitzGerald's initial candidates, Declan Costello, a High Court judge, and T.K. Whitaker, former secretary of the Department of Finance. Hume, realising that Haughey might veto any nominees from FitzGerald, asked his party colleague Hugh Logue for a suggestion. Logue proposed Colm Ó hEocha, the president of University College Galway and a respected academic. The other three leaders readily accepted Ó hEocha and he turned out to be a brilliant choice. I believe FitzGerald underestimated Ó hEocha's contribution to the success of the forum when he wrote in his autobiography, 'As chairman, he had the wisdom to employ a very loose rein in handling his four headstrong steeds.' Ó hEocha was subtle but firm in his style; he set a tone of civility and dignity in the public and private proceedings and the respect he earned helped to head off political divisions that threatened to undermine the forum at times. Hume and Spring also worked to ease tensions between FitzGerald and Haughey, who were so different in temperament, substance and political goals.

In keeping with the inter-party nature of the forum, the steering group appointed the diligent John (Jack) Tobin, Clerk of the Seanad, as secretary of the forum, with an independent secretariat seconded from the Department of the Taoiseach (Assistant Secretary Wally Kirwan was the indefatigable and able coordinator) and including

Richard O'Toole and Frank Sheridan from the Department of Foreign Affairs, Hugh Finlay from the National Board of Science and Technology, Colm Larkin from the EU Commission, and me from Government Information Services, where I was the deputy head on secondment from the Department of Foreign Affairs. Many of us as public servants were in uncharted waters, offering advice to and taking instructions from five bosses, a chairman and four party leaders. Ó hEocha championed the work of the secretariat, presenting our advice and research effectively to the steering group and to the forum meetings. I knew all the party leaders quite well, having worked for both FitzGerald and Haughey in the Department of the Taoiseach and having cooperated closely with Hume when I was press secretary for the Irish government in the United States (he frequently stayed in my apartment in New York and I had stayed with him in Derry). Dick Spring and I had been contemporaries at Trinity College.

With the Northern Ireland Assembly effectively in abeyance and the British government uncertain how to proceed, the political focus shifted to the forum, which opened formally in Dublin Castle on 30 May 1983, publishing its main report and an impressive eight sectoral reports a year later. In his opening speech, Hume addressed the unionists and the British government and British people, stressing that

> This Forum is not a nationalist conspiracy, neither is it a nationalist revival mission ... this is the most serious effort that has ever been made by Irish political leaders to face reality ... How would we propose to give to Unionists an adequate sense of security—physical, religious, political, economic and cultural—in a new Ireland?

(this and other quotes are taken from the public proceedings of the forum). FitzGerald said he had proposed the forum because 'we, the people of this State, have not sufficiently stirred ourselves to face reality ... so far as we are concerned, the agenda excludes nothing'. Haughey sought to narrow the options of the forum, stating that 'peace and stability cannot be secured without a withdrawal of the

British military and political presence from Northern Ireland'. He discussed 'some degree of autonomy for Northern Ireland' (which seemed to have more to do with avoiding changing laws in the south to accommodate unionists' views on divorce than anything else) and hoped for 'open minds on a variety of different political structures'. Dick Spring stated that as a socialist party, the Labour Party was pledged to 'the elimination of all sectarian laws, constitutional provisions and practices, both in the North and South, which are a major factor in dividing the working class'. He concluded by asking if the south was prepared to make changes 'if we are serious in our aspiration of Irish unity'.

In response to newspaper advertisements and solicitations, the forum received 317 submissions from both parts of Ireland, Great Britain, the United States, Belgium, France and Canada. Each party was entitled to invite a number of people to give oral presentations, which resulted in 31 individuals and groups speaking at 11 public meetings from 20 September 1983 to 9 February 1984. Fianna Fáil tended to invite groups and individuals who advocated a united Ireland (Seán MacBride, Desmond Fennell), whereas the other parties invited people and groups who would raise the uncomfortable unionist concerns that a new Ireland would have to address, including how to pay for a new Ireland, accommodate a British dimension both politically and culturally, and accomplish the separation of church and state. These included economics professor Louden Ryan, British Conservative politician Sir John Biggs-Davison, unionist politicians Christopher and Michael McGimpsey, Bernard Cullen and Richard Kearney (proposing joint sovereignty), and Alliance Party deputy leader Robin Glendinning.

RTÉ rendered an immense public service by providing live coverage of the presentations, helping to make Irish public opinion aware of the changes necessary to create an agreed Ireland. The Irish, British and American media were intrigued by the inter-party nature of the forum, which promised to make news, either in terms of a dramatic falling out among the parties or, as happened, a coming together on the realities and changes required for a new Ireland. Jon Nordheimer reported in the *New York Times* on the opening day of the forum that

It was Mr. Hume who posed the toughest challenges. 'I suggest that we begin by humbly admitting that no more difficult task ever confronted the Irish people. I suggest that we also understand clearly why we are attempting to do it—not because it would be gratifying to succeed, not because it would be interesting to attempt, not because it would be to our political advantage. Only because it would be dangerously irresponsible not to do this now.'

Since independence, the south, mostly concerned with its own economic and social issues, had been reluctant to become embroiled in the conflict in the north. Many of us as students had been deeply influenced by the civil rights movement in Northern Ireland and felt that the united Ireland mantra was a dead end that had both enabled British inaction for decades and empowered unionist discrimination against nationalists.

The widespread media coverage contributed immeasurably to the influence of the forum on audiences in Ireland, Britain and the United States. In addition to the very able journalists reporting for the Irish media, a number of talented journalists covered forum developments for British and American media, including Brendan Keenan for the *Financial Times*, Mary Holland for the *Observer* and Joe Joyce and Julia Langdon for the *Guardian*. Three renowned RTÉ journalists also consulted with the American television networks: Kevin Healy, NBC; Sean Duignan, CBS; and Mike Burns, ABC. Working with Sean Farrell, press counsellor at the Department of Foreign Affairs, and Pat Hennessy and Michael Collins, heads of press in the Irish embassies in London and Washington respectively, we invited editors from the British, European and American media to attend forum sessions and receive private briefings from party leaders.

My most enduring memory of the forum is the sense of goodwill and genuine enquiry that nearly every politician brought to the proceedings. The SDLP members patiently explained the realities of Northern Ireland to members from the south, many of whom had seldom been to Northern Ireland. What clearly united them, despite political and personality tensions among party leaders, members and the advisers, was the overwhelming imperative to stop the violence and killing in Northern Ireland and address its underlying causes. Nationalists in the north were becoming increasingly alienated and, unless something were to be done, the security of Ireland and Britain seemed seriously threatened. A sense of urgency, together with the sheer scale of the forum schedule—28 private sessions, 13 public sessions, 56 steering group meetings, plus sub-group meetings—built a greater awareness of what sacrifices would have to be made to reach agreement on the island. After the fourth public session, *The Irish Times* wrote in editorial on 6 October: 'The variety and cogency of the arguments so far heard justify the existence of the forum as a structure for getting the country's thoughts on the nature of Irish society, and Ireland's constitutional and political future in order.' Brendan Keenan reported in the *Financial Times* on 22 August that the forum was considering three major constitutional options, noting that 'some of the early doubt and cynicism about the body has lessened in the face of evidence that the politicians taking part are treating it seriously'. The article concluded: 'It is still possible that the Forum will fail to reach agreement, however, the general feeling is that the damage this would do, particularly to the SDLP, is so great that the politicians simply cannot afford to fail.' In his 1984 biography of John Hume (p. 256), Barry White observed: 'The documentation of the Forum was intended to be the most comprehensive review of Irish partition which had ever been done, with a value for the future of Anglo-Irish relations, which would long outlast the deliberations.'

Haughey more than most seemed determined to assert his prerogative as co-leader of the forum, angrily describing one secretariat paper as a 'non-paper' because he disagreed with its contents. On another occasion he forbade television coverage of a public presentation by the Women's Law and Research Group because it claimed that women's rights were better protected in the north. During the group's presentation, Haughey walked over to the secretariat table and muttered, 'Who invited these harridans?' He was always sensitive about media coverage and seemed in two minds about the amount of media coverage I encouraged. One morning, when I had given the BBC permission to film members arriving at Dublin Castle, he became furious and demanded to know why I had not consulted him first. I replied that I had consulted the chair and did not think it necessary to clear everything with the party leaders. That evening, by way of apparent apology, he sought me out to discuss some of the history of the castle. But he had laid down a marker: 'I too am your boss.'

A forum delegation from the four participating parties visited the north on 26–27 September 1983 and met groups representing a wide range of opinion, despite Ian Paisley's threat to prevent any such development. The only incident was at the Everglades Hotel outside Derry before one of the meetings. Hume and a few of us had arrived early at the hotel but when Seamus Mallon and others drove in, they were attacked in the car park by a group of Paisleyites with wooden staves. The delegates made it to the hotel lobby bruised and angry, but Hume urged everyone to be calm and not to allow the attackers to hijack the news coverage of the positive discussions under way. To add insult to injury, a day later when I was driving Mallon down to Dublin, we were stopped near Newry by UDR members who, despite clearly knowing who he was, insisted that he get out of the car to be identified.

Forum delegates also visited London for consultations in January 1984 with four of the major political parties. The public presentation by the Roman Catholic delegation on 9 February 1984 was another first, as political leaders questioned Catholic bishops in a public setting: a situation so unprecedented that the entire island was riveted to the live broadcasts of the proceedings. Bishop Cahal Daly stated that the Catholic Church

> have not sought and we do not seek a Catholic State for a Catholic people. We believe that the alliance of Church and State is harmful for the Church and harmful for the State … the Catholic Church in Ireland has no power and seeks no power except the power of the gospel.

He continued: 'We do feel bound to alert the consciences of Catholics to the moral and social evils which, as experience elsewhere shows, follow from certain kinds of legislative enactment,' adding that 'Divorce may cause more problems than those it seeks to control.' Senator Mary Robinson commented in the Seanad that 'witnessing the Catholic bishops and their representatives being questioned by politicians at the forum may have marked a modest beginning to a healthy separation of Church and State in Ireland'.

The 41-page forum report finally published on 2 May 1984 provided a breakthrough nationalist consensus of what a new Ireland would require. The report, accurately reflecting what the forum had heard over the previous year, noted the three elements that unionists wished to preserve: Britishness, Protestantism and the economic advantages of the British link (in the past, nationalists might have breezily responded that the unionists were really Irish, citing Irish Protestant rebels such as Wolfe Tone and Robert Emmet). As John Hume put it two years later (in *Ireland in the contemporary world*, edited by James Dooge):

> The Forum laid out a set of criteria which should be met by any initiative aimed at bringing progress towards peace and stability in Ireland and outlined three possible models which would meet those criteria. The heart of our approach was summed up in the following proposition: The solution to both the historic problem and the current crisis of Northern Ireland and the continuing problems of relations between Ireland and Britain necessarily requires new structures that will accommodate together two sets of legitimate rights:
>
> - the right of nationalists to effective political, symbolic and administrative expression of their identity; and
> - the right of unionists to effective political, symbolic and administrative expression of their identity, their ethos and their way of life.

Significantly, the concept of parity of esteem that was to underpin the Anglo-Irish Agreement and the 1998 Good Friday Agreement was clearly defined in the forum report:

The validity of both the nationalist and the unionist identities in Ireland and the democratic rights of
every citizen on this island must be accepted: both
of these identities must have equally satisfactory,
secure and durable, political, administrative and
symbolic expression and protection.

In the report as well, democratic Irish nationalism fully subscribed
to the consent of a majority in the north, accepting that 'agreement
means that the political arrangements for a new and sovereign
Ireland would have to be freely negotiated and agreed to by the
people of the North and by the people of the South'.

When the report was published, many observers focused less
on the radical new criteria and more on the prescriptive solution
preferred by the forum, which stated, 'The particular structure of
political unity which the Forum would wish to see established is a
unitary state.' Haughey had made the selection of only a unitary
state a make-or-break issue for Fianna Fáil, fearing no doubt that
his republican flank was exposed to Sinn Féin, whose electoral
gains had resulted in him losing power in 1981. SDLP deputy
leader Seamus Mallon supported Haughey, dismissing the idea of
presenting three options to the British as a 'dolly mixture' letting
them choose what they wanted. The other party leaders wanted
to offer three options but, feeling that there was value in securing
Fianna Fáil's support for the dramatic new assessment of nationalist and unionist rights, they agreed to a compromise indicating
a preference for the unitary state, and adding that two additional
'structural arrangements were examined in some detail—a federal/
confederal state and joint authority'. The three final chapters of
the report discussed these options at equal length. Importantly, the
report concluded, 'The Parties in the Forum also remain open to
discuss other views which may contribute to political development.'

The initial failure by some commentators to appreciate the
forum's new assessment of equality between unionists and nationalists together with nationalist willingness to discuss other political
structures was undoubtedly due to Haughey's press conference at
the conclusion of the forum, when he misquoted the report, stating
'the only solution is as stated in the report: a unitary state with a

new constitution'. He also rejected the consent agreed in the forum report, saying 'Nobody is entitled to deny the natural unity is unification of Ireland.' Most of the media coverage provided a balanced view of the report, but *Magill* magazine ran a front cover reading 'How Charlie swung the forum'. Unbeknown to the media, Irish government officials were already engaged in serious discussions with British officials on the basis of the new nationalist consensus regarding the rights of unionists and nationalists to equal treatment. They were also exploring joint sovereignty and joint authority, which discussions ultimately led to a new consultative role for Dublin in Northern Ireland as is discussed in later chapters.

A *Times* column written by former British education secretary Shirley Williams (4 May) recognised the forum report's achievement: 'It goes further than the nationalist parties have ever gone before in recognizing and respecting the unionist identity and Protestant ethos as being as valid a part of the Irish tradition as the nationalist identity and Catholic ethos.' On 2 June, a special *Economist* survey, 'The trouble with Ulster', concluded:

> For Britain, the joint authority route is a gamble worth taking because the prize—unlike 1969 and 1972—is lower cost and a reduced (or initially shared) British involvement. It in no way offends the guarantee, although Mr. Paisley will say it does. The guarantee remains the top tier of Ulster sovereignty. Beneath it, a joint authority composed of Dublin and London ministers, but gradually embracing Ulster leaders too, might also concern itself with Mr. FitzGerald's shopping list: economics and trade, agriculture and tourism, issues which are naturally all-Ireland in character.

Although *Economist* articles have no bylines, this survey owed much to political editor Simon Jenkins and home affairs editor Frances Cairncross, who, like their colleague Brenda Maddox, followed Irish affairs closely.

In an interim response in July, Northern Ireland Secretary of State James Prior accepted 'the positive value' in the forum's examination of nationalist aspirations, its emphasis on the importance of consent, its attempt to understand the unionist identity and its openness to discuss other views. FitzGerald used his power as taoiseach to begin to sell the emerging forum consensus to the United States, including in an address to a joint session of the US Congress on 15 March. The *New York Times* (24 November) noted that Prime Minister FitzGerald's 'Irish Forum broke new ground by proposing not only North–South union or confederation but acknowledging Protestant claims to British identity. It offered a third-choice compromise of "joint authority" —letting both Britain's and Ireland's flags fly in Northern Ireland.' In addition, President Reagan's trip to Ireland in June provided a valuable opportunity to influence his thinking, especially given that, as Seán Donlon noted, Reagan's pressure on Thatcher proved to be pivotal in Dublin–London negotiations during the following months.

While it was politically embarrassing for FitzGerald to be taunted by Haughey after the infamous 'out, out, out' comments by Thatcher (Haughey referred to 'the Britshit Prime Minister' in the Dáil exchange with FitzGerald, but then withdrew the remark), *The Times* noted on 21 November that 'the analysis of Northern Ireland's disorders offered in the forum report is endorsed by the British government to a significant extent'. The editorial referred to this analysis, which became part of the language of the summit communique, as 'Forumese'. The secretary of the British Cabinet, Sir Robert Armstrong, astutely noted later that 'with its reexamination of the aspirations of Irish nationalism, the New Ireland Forum Report gave him [FitzGerald] an opportunity to go into negotiations with somewhat more room for maneuver than he might otherwise have had'. Armstrong also observed that in 1983, FitzGerald and Thatcher 'had won elections and enjoyed the prospect of four years in office', offering a rare timeline to sign and implement a new political initiative without electoral disruption (see *Northern Ireland and the politics of reconciliation*, edited by Dermot Keogh and Michael Haltzel, pp 205–6).

The eminent historian J.J. Lee noted the historical importance of the forum—'The influence of the Forum can be detected in the analysis of the situation underlying the [Anglo-Irish] Agreement'— especially in proposing equality of identity as the solution and in accepting that unionists would have no veto on policy formulation within Northern Ireland (*Ireland 1912–1985: politics and society*, pp 681–2). It took imagination and political courage to redefine Irish nationalism, without which there would have been no Anglo-Irish Agreement; almost certainly the spiral of violence would have increased, leading to the breakdown of society in Ireland: a breakdown we have witnessed in many other countries that have failed to overcome differences. In retrospect, it is clear that the twelve months devoted to the New Ireland Forum by leading politicians, civil servants, academics and the media provided the basis for the equality of the nationalist and unionist identities, a radical new departure on the long road to peace and equal rights in Ireland. Above all, FitzGerald, Hume and Spring had succeeded in widening the mandate of Irish nationalism, which greatly strengthened their hand in negotiations with Thatcher and the British government over the following years.

Panel 1 Overview

MARY E. DALY

The period covered by the contributions to this panel can be viewed as a time of remarkable progress in the development of an Irish policy on Northern Ireland, when the key structures and policies that ultimately resulted in the Good Friday Agreement evolved. Yet these years were marked by recurrent violence, security concerns, hunger strikes and little apparent progress in the search for peace and stability. Two of the contributors here, Seán Donlon and Noel Dorr, had first-hand experience of Northern Ireland policy over almost 30 years, from the late 1960s until the mid/late 1990s; they served as ambassadors to the USA and UK respectively, and as secretaries of the Department of Foreign Affairs (DFA). Their contributions capture the evolution of Irish government policy. The outbreak of violence in Northern Ireland in the summer of 1969 represented an existential crisis for the Irish government, which it was utterly unprepared to address. There was no government minister, no department, not even a solitary civil servant with responsibility for or expertise on Northern Ireland. In the early 1950s Irish diplomats had made occasional visits to Northern Ireland to maintain contact with northern nationalists, but the practice ended in September 1955, for reasons that are unclear. As shown in the latest volume of *Documents on Irish Foreign Policy* (vol. XI, document 251), in January 1960 Conor Cruise O'Brien, then a member of the DFA, suggested that these visits should be resumed, but that did not happen.

The process of re-establishing contacts with northern national-ists in 1969 began as a spontaneous initiative by Eamonn Gallagher of the DFA, without any formal approval. He made regular visits to family in Donegal, stopping off in Derry on the way to meet John Hume. His reports proved critical to the development of govern-ment policy. Noel Dorr, on holiday in Ireland in the summer of 1969, went into Iveagh House to help with press briefings. In 1971 Seán Donlon was recalled from Boston for a temporary assignment to investigate the treatment of internees; he spent most of the next seven years travelling in Northern Ireland, developing contacts with politicians and community leaders, initially on the nationalist side. The DFA had to improve its communications and press strategy, arranging briefings and visits for foreign journalists to communi-cate the Irish point of view. It was a matter of all hands on deck: Noel Dorr, technically an official in the press unit, contributed to the evolving policy on Northern Ireland, writing speeches for Taoiseach Jack Lynch.

By 1973 the structures and core policies that shaped the Northern Ireland peace process were in place: the joint responsibil-ity of the Department of the Taoiseach and Department of Foreign Affairs; the importance of building contacts with politicians and civil society; the emphasis on human rights —as evidenced in the Strasbourg case. When the Troubles began in 1969 British ministers rejected any Irish involvement, yet within a relatively short time, Ireland had persuaded the British government that it had a legiti-mate role in Northern Ireland policy. The Sunningdale Agreement of December 1973—providing for a power-sharing executive in Northern Ireland and a Council of Ireland, with an all-island executive 'and harmonising functions and a consultative role'— reflected a remarkable evolution in Irish and British thinking. But the agreement collapsed within months; Noel Dorr, author of the definitive book on Sunningdale, has described it as 'half-baked'.

Following the collapse of the power-sharing executive, there were fears that the British Labour government might withdraw from Northern Ireland. Wally Kirwan, who worked closely on Northern Ireland policy with Dermot Nally in the Department of the Taoiseach, speaking from the floor, explained that much of the mid-1970s was spent 'dealing with disaster scenarios ... The

Department of Defence was working out how many refugees we could manage. We were looking at the politics of an independent Northern Ireland.' There was no real prospect of progress during the years of the IRA prisoner hunger strikes, but Andy O'Rourke, a former secretary of the DFA, speaking from the floor, emphasised that the department worked to maintain contacts with its British counterpart.

Irish-America offered a more constructive forum, and Ted Smyth, press attaché at the Irish embassy in Washington, worked with ambassador Seán Donlon and Michael Lillis to develop a support network on Capitol Hill, and to overcome the long-standing silence of US presidents on Northern Ireland. The Carter statement of 30 August 1977—expressing support for peaceful means to secure a just solution in Northern Ireland that would establish a form of government commanding the acceptance of both parts of the community, protecting human rights and guaranteeing freedom from discrimination, plus a commitment of US investment funds—provided the framework for later US involvement in the Northern Ireland peace process.

The New Ireland Forum was an attempt to generate new ideas about Northern Ireland against the backdrop of growing support for Sinn Féin, and an apparent lack of interest by Britain in policy towards Northern Ireland other than security initiatives. It was the first occasion since the Irish Convention of 1917–18 that nationalism, unionism and possible constitutional settlements were discussed on an all-Ireland basis. Although Ulster unionist politicians refused to take part, Hugh Logue, a member of the forum, speaking from the floor, suggested that 'It engaged some of the more enlightened unionist community in the north and a number of them came to give their views to the forum, and I think that helped to open a dialogue there.' He also recalled the work done by the forum on the economic impact of north–south cooperation.

Ted Smyth, a member of the forum secretariat, highlighted the language used in the forum report: the need for 'new structures that will accommodate together two sets of legitimate rights: the right of Nationalists to effective political, symbolic and administrative expression of their identity and the right of Unionists to effective political, symbolic and administrative expression of their identity, their ethos and their way of life'. He suggested that this language 'still stands up today'. Frank Sheridan, a member of the forum secretariat, speaking from the floor, noted the value of televising the public sessions of the forum, and its importance in shifting momentum in both London and Ireland. Unionist speakers conveyed a clear message to the forum that Irish unification by coercion or persuasion was not a likely prospect, which helped pave the way for the 1985 Anglo-Irish Agreement.

Mid-1980s and Onwards:
Anglo-Irish Agreement and
Secretariat at Maryfield

—

The Anglo-Irish Agreement of 1985

MICHAEL LILLIS

When Garret FitzGerald was elected taoiseach in November 1982, the state of Anglo-Irish relations was, as he says in his autobiography, 'little short of disastrous'. Two British administrations, those of Harold Wilson and Margaret Thatcher, had since the collapse of Sunningdale in 1974 concentrated their priorities—without success—on defeating the IRA and had abjured all efforts to make political progress, believing such initiatives to be impracticable or even counterproductive. They had thus, in practice, accepted a unionist veto on any proposals for the future of Northern Ireland emanating from Dublin or constitutional nationalists in Northern Ireland, thereby ensuring impermeable unionist hegemony and nationalist despair. Mrs Thatcher and her team had woefully mismanaged the challenges of the hunger strikes, entrenching the alienation of the minority community—even of the majority within that community that opposed the violence of the Provisional IRA. For most nationalists in Northern Ireland and for many in the south, Mrs Thatcher had come to epitomise the worst of British antipathy and inhumanity.

The brief glimmer of hope at the time of Mr Haughey's 'teapot summit' with Mrs Thatcher in 1981 had been quenched almost immediately by the over-selling by some Dublin ministers of what, at first sight, had seemed an ingenious and fecund phrase in a communiqué—'the totality of relations'. This was unfortunately represented as somehow portending a willingness on the part of Mrs Thatcher to support Irish unity. Her unconcealed rage had virtually closed down all exchanges with Dublin. The taoiseach fatally decided in 1982 to use Ireland's temporary membership of the UN Security Council to try to frustrate Mrs Thatcher's Falklands War at a time of high military uncertainty. This had put the final kibosh on any hope for the slightest dialogue between Dublin and London, much less any political progress. Meanwhile loyalist terrorists continued their butchery of innocent Catholics with the suspected (and subsequently proven) connivance of sections of the security forces, while the Provisional IRA extended its 'long war', killing and maiming and destroying economic opportunity and hope throughout Ireland. Each set of extremists believed, alas with some plausibility, that their respective hopes for chaos were enhanced. Minister for Foreign Affairs Peter Barry's memorable description, 'the nightmare of the northern nationalists', was extending across the island of Ireland.

I was recalled from temporary service with the European Commission and given responsibility at official level for Anglo-Irish affairs in the Department of Foreign Affairs at this bleak juncture. I found myself in the middle of an intense emergency planning exercise between the new taoiseach, Garret FitzGerald, and SDLP leader John Hume. I knew both men reasonably well, having been the taoiseach's diplomatic adviser in his short-lived administration of 1981–82 and having worked closely with Hume both in Northern Ireland and earlier in Washington, DC, on President Carter's initiative on Northern Ireland, 1976–7. Their working relationship was extraordinarily candid both politically and intellectually: they met regularly in Dublin, usually at the taoiseach's home. Otherwise I travelled to Hume's house in the Bogside on most weekends with a list of suggestions and queries from Dr FitzGerald, reporting back on Sunday evening or Monday.

They planned a two-part strategy: first, a redefinition of principles through the New Ireland Forum, which they hoped to use as a new agenda for an approach to London; and second, a scoping out of the ground in Mrs Thatcher's government to prepare our interlocutors there for this fresh approach. The forum discussions between the SDLP and the parties in the Dáil proved to be a highly creative and permanently valuable exercise: its generous analysis of the Irish nationalist and British unionist identities and its definitions of the principles for creating a new Ireland (consent, mutual acceptance, non-violence) have hardly been improved on since, even in the Good Friday Agreement, and could with benefit be revisited today.

The success of the forum in terms of FitzGerald's and Hume's objectives of providing an agenda for discussion with Thatcher was, however, frustrated by the public insistence of Mr Haughey (sincere, if erroneous, I believed) that the exclusive focus of the forum should be not on those principles, but on the promotion of a unitary Irish state, which would of course immediately void any possibility of opening a dialogue with Mrs Thatcher at that time. As the situation in Northern Ireland continued to fester, it became urgent to devise a new tack.

FitzGerald and Hume understood that the only possible agenda from which to launch any serious discussion with Thatcher was to engage with her obsession with security policy. Nothing else would even begin to get a hearing. 'Security policy' did not mean 'neutrality'—or NATO-related scenarios—which, though much hyped in some circles in Dublin in those years, had no attraction whatever for her, but rather the elimination of terrorism on the ground as the only route to some form of stability. Even though she didn't, or wasn't prepared to, see it as such, it was obvious that the main source of support for the IRA was the rising alienation of the Catholic community in Northern Ireland provoked by the failed policies of successive British governments over the previous eight years and their deliberate occlusion of any political agenda.

The taoiseach's putative argument to Mrs Thatcher, as elaborated in close cooperation with Hume, would in summary have run as follows.

> You [British] have failed and there is nothing in your current political/security arsenal that will help achieve stability. Alas, only the contrary is inevitable politically and economically in Northern Ireland. We respectfully believe that you need

our help. Only the involvement of the political resources of the Irish state, our security forces, our judicial system and our active input into the system of government of Northern Ireland can arrest and reverse the alienation and despair of the minority and bring them to identify with and accept a system of political/security authority. The people in the Irish state have no desire for this role. We propose this reluctantly and because we on our side of the border have been suffering since the collapse of Sunningdale in 1974, and are continuing to suffer, the destructive consequences politically and economically of British failures of policy on the other side. (The special study by the forum 'The cost of violence' provides a dramatic and well-researched reminder of the economic damage and loss of opportunity in the south as well as in the north.) This is not an agenda for nationalist utopia: we propose it because we believe that it is *necessary* for the security and stability of Northern Ireland and its people, for the security and economic prosperity of our own state and, frankly, for your security and political interests, both domestically and internationally.

Both FitzGerald and Hume also foresaw that inevitably Britain would demand a willingness on the part of the Irish government to be prepared to change the territorial claims in articles 2 and 3 of our constitution, which, if the Irish démarche produced a credible reaction of interest, would consequently require serious consideration.

It was obvious that this argument could not be presented in private, much less in public, by the taoiseach to this prime minister at this time: her reaction would predictably be outrage and we would probably be driven back to where we had started, if not further. Much less could it be announced publicly by the Irish government or the SDLP to deeply sceptical and alienated nationalist opinion either in the north or in the south. So, a personal opinion, confidentially but sincerely expressed by a 'subaltern' and publicly obscure official, but one who could credibly represent the taoiseach's personal thinking (though not necessarily yet that of his government), to a similarly placed British official (that is, one close to the prime minister) might provide a stimulus to promote the beginning of serious dialogue. Or not, as the case might be. At least it should not make matters worse.

One valuable legacy of Mr Haughey's 'teapot' summitry was a structure for promoting dialogue between London and Dublin at summit, ministerial and working levels. It had withered somewhat under the pressure of intervening events, but FitzGerald set about reviving it at the highest level of both civil services by dispatching the secretary to the Irish government, Dermot Nally, to meet the British Cabinet secretary, Sir Robert Armstrong. Nally and Armstrong, men of remarkable intellectual gifts, of Job-like patience, unflagging good humour, self-deprecating modesty and determined courage, had maintained a relationship of mutual trust and esteem throughout the vicissitudes of appalling events. They have created noble legacies, both severally and together, in the history of Anglo-Irish relations.

They appointed Deputy Cabinet Secretary Sir David Goodall, a senior diplomat seconded from the Foreign and Commonwealth Office, and myself as co-chairmen of a coordinating committee, to work with the ministries and departments of the respective governments to develop projects to promote practical cooperation between the two administrations in fields such as agriculture, health, education and welfare. The original theory, as envisaged in the earlier Anglo-Irish summits, was that this work would, in the buzzwords of 1981, 'thicken' and otherwise enhance the 'totality of relations' through 'joint studies' between the two administrations.

And so on 8 September 1983 Goodall (whom I had met in London briefly) and I met in Dublin with teams from the respective departments of Health and Education to agree a programme of work aimed at developing further the mutual recognition of degrees and qualifications for nurses and doctors. Together with our colleagues we had a working session and then a pleasant lunch in the Grey Door restaurant on Pembroke Street. Goodall takes up the story in an article published, in tandem with a parallel recollection of my own, in the internet journal *Dublin Review of Books* 27 years later:

> So it was a complete surprise when, at the first meeting of our co-ordinating committee in September 1983 in Dublin, Michael Lillis invited me to take a quiet walk with him along the Grand Canal and proceeded to sketch out the possibility of radically new arrangements for Northern Ireland. He made it clear that these were not yet the ideas of the Irish government, but indicated that they were the lines on which the taoiseach was thinking.
>
> No two interlocutors approaching a subject from differing points of view ever carry away exactly the same understanding of what was said. With that qualification, my understanding from Michael of what the taoiseach was tentatively envisaging was unequivocal Irish acceptance of the Union, if necessary including amendment of Articles 2 and 3 of the constitution, and a revived Northern Ireland parliament, in return for an Irish political presence in the North together with the participation of Irish police and security forces in operations there and of Irish judges in terrorist trials. This stemmed from a recognition that unification was not a realistic goal for the foreseeable future; and that unless the Catholic minority in the North could be brought to identify themselves with the institutions of law and order there (from which they were profoundly and increasingly alienated), Sinn Féin would replace the SDLP as the legitimate representative of the nationalist community, with disastrous consequences for the island of Ireland as a whole. The taoiseach accordingly believed that outright acceptance of the Union would be a price worth paying for measures that, by addressing Northern nationalists' concerns, would end their alienation from the institutions of the state in the

North and demonstrate that constitutional—that is non-violent—nationalism could achieve more for nationalists than Sinn Féin and the IRA.

Having had no previous dealings with Michael Lillis, and being a newcomer to the Anglo-Irish political scene, I was uncertain what to make of these (to me) astonishingly far-reaching ideas and not sure how far they were to be taken seriously. I also had some difficulty in believing that I had been chosen as the channel for conveying to London a major new initiative by the taoiseach. But Michael Lillis, while leaving me in no doubt that he was by background and conviction a strong and emotional Irish nationalist with his fair share of historic resentments about the British role in Ireland, impressed me as being honest, intelligent and capable of being both imaginative and objective. While I thought that any idea of Irish troops or police operating in the North would be a non-starter in London, it seemed to me that unequivocal Irish acceptance of the Union, confirmed by the amendment of Articles 2 and 3, might be a step of sufficient symbolic and political importance to justify the introduction of an 'Irish dimension' of some kind into the Northern Ireland administration. So I duly reported my understanding of what Michael Lillis had said.

This report engaged Mrs Thatcher's interest. But it was received in Whitehall with scepticism, and subsequent exploratory encounters at various levels were needed to establish that these were in fact the taoiseach's ideas.

A series of probing meetings with Goodall followed over several weeks in Dublin, London and Oxford. The pro-unionist Northern Ireland Office (NIO) in particular found the Irish ideas and their source to be both objectionable and unhinged (a neologism, 'Lillisisms', became current around Whitehall). Nevertheless, the taoiseach confirmed to Armstrong in a private meeting in

Dublin in late October that Lillis had indeed faithfully represented his thinking. He again confirmed this to Mrs Thatcher at a summit meeting in Chequers on 7 November 1983. This gave rise to a marathon Anglo-Irish negotiation led by the respective cabinet secretaries (the 'Nally–Armstrong talks'), beginning almost immediately and culminating in the signature of the Anglo-Irish Agreement on 15 November 1985. Meetings alternated on a six-weekly basis—sometimes more frequently—between Ireland and England; sometimes in government offices, sometimes in secluded country houses. There were 35 sessions in all, mostly lasting two days but sometimes longer.

Until 28 September 1984 the British team comprised Armstrong and Goodall only. The Irish side had not at any point requested the exclusion of the NIO; nevertheless, its absence was read by our side as inevitably requiring the approval of Margaret Thatcher and thus as an earnest of a serious new departure by London. By the time the highly sceptical head of the NIO and three colleagues had been added, the talks had gathered a momentum that it would have been difficult to arrest without a public explosion. This did not deter the NIO team from trying repeatedly and strenuously to arrange such an outcome.

The Irish team, led by Dermot Nally, comprised Seán Donlon, secretary of DFA, deeply experienced like Dermot Nally in Anglo-Irish negotiations, including at Sunningdale and—crucially—personally influential with President Reagan and his White House; Noel Dorr, ambassador in London where his access across the British government was most useful, also ex-Sunningdale with a crucially valuable gift (matched collaboratively by Armstrong) for finding ingenious solutions to drafting impasses in Anglo-Irish exchanges, and with a compendious set of historical and philosophical convictions on Anglo-Irish relations; and myself. Later Andrew Ward, secretary of the Department of Justice, was added: his was the most brilliant mind I encountered in a lifetime of negotiation in the public and (more recently) private sectors. Declan Quigley, a genial and learned barrister (expert on articles 2 and 3!) and head of the attorney general's office, joined also.

The principal protagonists were Mrs Thatcher and Garret FitzGerald and their meetings and correspondence were the crucial exchanges of the whole process. The taoiseach's task was enormous and sometimes wearisome. Most encounters had to commence from scratch, if not further back: Mrs Thatcher kept reverting to the Sudetenland Germans in 1930s Czechoslovakia, in arguing that minorities had basically no rights. We learned that in her internal consultations she had even urged a consideration of repeating Cromwell's dispersal of the Irish to Connaught (or to Hell!) by removing, on that very precedent, the Catholics across the border from Northern Ireland. FitzGerald persisted, however, exhibiting remarkable patience, courtesy and self-possession, and heroic tenacity. Armstrong and Goodall frequently advised that we should urge the taoiseach to be as clear and persistent as possible in his dealings with Mrs Thatcher. We learned that she regularly balked at the whole business, particularly after private consultations with her close friend and mentor Enoch Powell, her private secretary Charles Powell, and the NIO.

A review of the negotiations as a whole, including the reflections of the late David Goodall (he kept a fascinating and detailed journal that he kindly showed to me before he died three years ago), discloses a complex and somewhat bizarre political personality, especially when it came to Ireland. Her instincts were viscerally unionist; she instinctively disliked, if not hated, Irish nationalism; and her reflections even in private were frequently delivered in jingoistic terms as though to the front page of the *Sun* newspaper. Nevertheless, while often 'pretending' to misunderstand him, she gradually took FitzGerald's arguments to heart and, however reluctantly, signed an agreement that gave to the much disliked foreign state of which he was the political leader, for the first time since 1922, a treaty-based right to have a crucial role and a physical presence at the centre of the processes of the government of Northern Ireland. His achievement, in an almost Sisyphean marathon of diplomatic persuasion and psychology, would be hard to match: I can think of no equal for it. I believe that his wise wife, Joan, gave him much insightful counsel.

There were two other crucial factors. One was the unwearying, firm but gentle advocacy of Mrs Thatcher's Cabinet secretary, Robert Armstrong, for an agreement. I have just read Lady Antonia Fraser's gripping history of the British politics of Catholic emancipation,

The King and the Catholics: Fraser's account of the masterful persuasions by the Duke of Wellington versus the absolute refusal of King George IV to assent to Catholic emancipation legislation reminded me almost eerily of Armstrong's persistence, despite the uninterrupted efforts of the NIO and of the supporters of Mrs Thatcher's friend Enoch Powell to thwart Nally–Armstrong at all costs.

Another was undoubtedly the role of President Reagan. The background here is the persuasion by John Hume and the Four Horsemen (Speaker Tip O'Neill, Senators Kennedy and Moynihan and Governor Carey) and Irish diplomacy (led by Garret FitzGerald, then minister for foreign affairs) of President Jimmy Carter in 1977 to take the first US position on Northern Ireland independent of London since partition. That created a precedent. In 1984, at another moment of reluctance by Mrs Thatcher, Hume and Seán Donlon inspired Speaker O'Neill and Donlon's friends in the White House to persuade President Reagan to urge her to commit again to Anglo-Irish negotiations with FitzGerald. She personally acknowledged the role of the US in conversation with Lord McAlpine, the treasurer of the Conservative Party at that time, as confirmed in his autobiography and also in comments to Goodall recorded in his journal.

Two events in the public arena punctuated the otherwise secret negotiations (our side briefed John Hume, but only Hume, on the progress of the negotiations: he meticulously respected this condition throughout, though it created difficulties for him with his party).

The first was the bombing of the Grand Hotel in Brighton by the Provisional IRA on 12 October 1984, during the annual conference of the Conservative Party, which came very close to killing the prime minister and her husband and conceivably her entire Cabinet, and tragically killed or maimed several of her close friends and colleagues. The horror of this atrocity was such that many felt that she might suspend the Nally–Armstrong negotiations. To her credit, she ordered that they resume.

The second was Mrs Thatcher's public rejection of the three possible structures for a New Ireland proposed in the forum report, in her infamous 'out, out, out' press conference of 19 November 1984 following her quite substantive if combative summit earlier that day with Dr FitzGerald at Chequers. These were a unitary state, confederation or joint authority (see Ted Smyth's chapter in this volume). This drama caused extensive humiliation for the taoiseach in the Dáil and in public opinion throughout nationalist Ireland, and seriously destabilised the momentum of the negotiations (my own back gave out at this point and I noted a line from one of Ó Rathaille's most tormented lyrics about the British in my own journal: *Is fada liom oíche fhíor-fhliuch gan suan gan srann*).

FitzGerald bore the opprobrium with almost inhuman silent patience, prophesying correctly to his advisers that she would have to compensate for her (largely unintended, if typical) blunder. Mrs Thatcher was in due course forced to make several conciliatory gestures, not least in confirming, at the instance of President Reagan, in her address in February 1985 to a joint session of the US Congress that she was committed to her negotiations with Dr FitzGerald.

The Anglo-Irish Agreement that finally emerged on 15 November 1985 was different in a number of ways from both the Sunningdale Agreement and the Good Friday Agreement. Its main institutional objective was radical and unprecedented: to facilitate a major 'intrusive' role for the Irish government in the processes of government within Northern Ireland through a treaty-based system of cooperation between the two governments in all political, social and economic matters; cultural and human-rights issues (including parades and processions); and security issues, including reform of the security forces, cross-border security cooperation and measures to reform the judiciary. The mechanism to give effect to the role of Dublin was the treaty provision whereby the Irish government could put forward views (including investigative queries) and proposals across this entire agenda, and the corresponding provision that the British assumed an obligation to join in 'determined efforts to resolve any differences in the interest of peace and security'.

By the end of the Nally–Armstrong negotiation the British demand that the Irish government change articles 2 and 3 of the constitution in return for the British concessions in the agreement had been diluted to a treaty-based joint statement of recognition of the political reality. During the negotiations, British ministers—notably Douglas Hurd, secretary of state for Northern Ireland—and the senior officials of the Northern Ireland Office had trapped themselves by arguing condescendingly that it would be an unconscionable risk for Dublin to hazard an uncertain referendum on these issues: their intent being to narrow the agenda and intrusiveness of the role of the Irish government; in this they mainly failed. My personal conviction at the time, for what a civil servant's unpolitical authority is worth, was that the taoiseach Garret FitzGerald, the tánaiste Dick Spring and the minister for foreign affairs Peter Barry would have been ready to put the agreement to the people in the south as sufficient counterpoint to adjusting article 2 from a territorial claim on Northern Ireland to an aspiration to Irish unity by agreement (as happened in 1998 following the Good Friday Agreement). In fact, despite the opposition of Mr Haughey, leader of the Fianna Fáil opposition in the Dáil, the agreement was approved by over 70 per cent in opinion polls in the south, and the enthusiastic support of Hume, Mallon and the SDLP enhanced its popularity. The evident satisfaction of nationalist opinion in the north, mirrored by loyalist and unionist outrage at the time, undoubtedly (if not ideally!) buttressed the credibility of the agreement for the southern electorate. One can today retrospectively regret that an opportunity was perhaps lost to reconcile at least some unionist opinion by meeting their visceral demand that the south withdraw what they saw as its constitutional territorial claim. Naturally, once the British themselves had desisted from demanding constitutional change, while conceding an extensive role to Dublin across the entire agenda of internal government in Northern Ireland, the Irish side had no immediate need to maintain a commitment to constitutional change.

The agreement reprised, but for the first time in treaty language, the Sunningdale principle that there would be no change in the status of Northern Ireland without the consent of a majority of the people of Northern Ireland. It did so not in separate British and Irish statements, as at Sunningdale, but in a *joint* assertion. Significantly, it added a specific commitment in article 1 (c) in which both governments declared that 'if in the future a majority of the people of Northern Ireland clearly wish for and formally consent to the establishment of a united Ireland, *they will introduce and support in the respective Parliaments legislation to give effect to that wish'* (emphasis added). This treaty-based confirmation that Britain had no 'selfish' interest in 'occupying' Northern Ireland was the central argument adduced thereafter by John Hume to persuade Gerry Adams (and through him the leaders of Sinn Féin and the Provisional IRA) that there could be no nationalist justification whatever for their campaign of violence. In article 1(b) both sides for the first time recognised the reality at that time 'that the present wish of a majority of the people of Northern Ireland is for no change in the status of Northern Ireland'.

The origins of much, though by no means all, of the 1985 agreement can be traced to Sunningdale and the lessons from its collapse in 1974 in the face of the loyalist workers' strike. For example, an objective of the negotiators of the 1985 agreement was that the institutions they created should be 'non-boycottable': this meant in practice non-boycottable by unionists and loyalists. Curiously, but significantly, this was never formally stated as an objective between the two sets of negotiators. It was, nevertheless, well understood from the beginning and it was of course achieved. Mrs Thatcher and her government—and most significantly the RUC—came under sustained violent loyalist pressure to resile from the agreement but they stood firmly behind it.

Another key objective, shared and positively acknowledged by both sides, was to facilitate and encourage power-sharing between unionists and nationalists, rather than making the establishment of power-sharing a precondition for the agreement itself to function. In this respect both Sunningdale and the later Good Friday Agreement were different. The 1985 agreement did, however, provide, as an inducement to unionists to take part, the carrot-and-stick contrivance whereby any issues that might be agreed by unionists and nationalists for power-sharing in Northern Ireland would be removed from the remit and agenda of the Dublin–London intergovernmental council, thus in theory reducing or eventually removing Dublin's hated 'interference'.

For the Dublin team and particularly for the taoiseach, Garrret FitzGerald, another key but 'unspoken' objective was to push its terms as closely as possible to a system of joint authority between Dublin and London for the government of Northern Ireland. I say 'unspoken' in this case (as in several others!) because we were painfully aware that any specific mention by us of 'joint authority' as a non-negotiable minimum objective would have automatically torpedoed the negotiations for the British team: Mrs Thatcher emphatically did not recognise any fundamental distinction or indeed any distinction whatever between joint authority, which the taoiseach argued did not impinge on sovereignty, and joint sovereignty, which was anathema to her. The result was that we had to aim for as much of the substance—as opposed to the form—of joint authority as we could achieve in practice. In fact the Anglo-Irish Agreement proved to be remarkably intrusive into the processes of government of Northern Ireland.

The Anglo-Irish Agreement was almost immediately ratified by the Dáil and the House of Commons. Richard Ryan recounts the extraordinary efforts of our diplomacy in London, which conciliated many hitherto doubtful Tory grandees and backwoodsmen to an agreement that many unionists saw as a shocking betrayal by their talisman, Margaret Thatcher.

Fianna Fáil under Mr Haughey's leadership opposed the agreement in the Dáil. John Hume viewed this as a disastrous loss of opportunity to persuade the Provisional IRA to cease its campaign by a united effort at persuasion strengthened by the treaty guarantees on Irish unity of article 1. A small number of Mr Haughey's adherents seceded from his party, forming the Progressive Democrats (PDs). When Mr Haughey returned to power in 1987, far from repudiating the agreement as he had threatened, he worked its mechanisms assiduously. The Provisional IRA intensified its campaign of violence.

The unionist and loyalist reactions were convulsed and hysterical, as epitomised by the Reverend Paisley's rallying roar to a mass Belfast protest: 'We say never, never, never.' Over time a reconsideration set in and led to the Good Friday Agreement of 1998. It was a condition of that agreement that, in a key concession to Ulster unionist leader David Trimble, the Anglo-Irish Agreement of 1985 was formally abrogated. Nevertheless the substance and language of the 1985 agreement are fully preserved in Strand 3 of the Good Friday Agreement.

I readily acknowledge that the 1985 agreement had shortcomings. Perhaps most notable was the fact that, despite the clear intentions set out in article 8 and the efforts of Mrs Thatcher, it proved impossible for the British side to deliver any concrete result. Article 8 provided that:

> the two Governments agree on the importance of public confidence in the administration of justice. The Conference shall seek, with the advice from experts as appropriate, measures which would give substantial expression to this aim, considering inter alia the possibility of mixed courts in both jurisdictions for the trial of certain offences.

This failure was due to the obdurate resistance of Lord Chancellor Hailsham, whose office at that time had constitutional independence from the UK government (this was adjusted under the later Blair administration), to introducing 'mixed' courts from both jurisdictions in Ireland for terrorist trials (the 'security' benefits of which Mrs Thatcher clearly appreciated) or even to institute a three-judge court system in Northern Ireland. In this obduracy Hailsham was joined by the then chief justice of Northern Ireland, Lord Lowry. No such reforms have since been instituted, even under the Good Friday Agreement or St Andrews' arrangements. This seems a pity.

I don't think an intergovernmental project similar to the Anglo-Irish Agreement has been attempted for the government of any other area in the world that, like Northern Ireland, was disputed between two states and subject to intercommunal strife. The most obvious analogous opportunity is Kashmir, long disputed in inter-state violence between India and Pakistan and in inter-community violence on the ground. It happened that David Goodall was appointed British high commissioner in New Delhi following the conclusion of the Anglo-Irish Agreement. He subsequently lamented the fact that, despite his own quiet urging, such were the hostile relations between the two countries that an arrangement akin to the Anglo-Irish Agreement was beyond their respective or combined diplomatic competences.

An important structural difference between the Anglo-Irish Agreement and Sunningdale was that Sunningdale was significantly focused on the (aborted) Council of Ireland as its north–south dimension. The Anglo-Irish Agreement was different because its Irish dimension was a project whereby the Irish government intruded into the government in Northern Ireland. We don't have this today. Sometimes, as I see the current political blockages in Belfast, I am tempted to wish that we had. Long-term speculation might envisage a transition aimed at securing unionist political security, if in the future a majority in the north were to opt for Irish unity, whereby the UK government could have a role in the Northern Ireland government within a sovereign all-Ireland structure similar to that of the Dublin government under the 1985 agreement. It's a possible scenario.

Some days after the Anglo-Irish Agreement was signed by the taoiseach and the prime minister, David Goodall and I and our families met for a quiet celebration at his flat in London, which by then I had got to know fairly well, as he had my own home in Dublin. We exchanged gifts. He gave me one of his celebrated watercolours—a view of Howth harbour in perfect tranquillity—and a piece of family silver fraternally inscribed. I gave him an original 1798 pike procured and validated by my friend the late Ronan Fanning, our most accomplished historian of Anglo-Irish relations. I had a little clasp affixed to the staff and inscribed to him *as Gaeilge*. Goodall was delighted: his Wexford ancestors had struggled on both sides of that rising, about which he knew a great deal. He expertly demonstrated to us there and then how to deploy the 'business end' of the implement. Later it hung over the fireplace in the British high commissioner's palatial residence in New Delhi.

Many officials in the Department of Foreign Affairs unmentioned above worked assiduously, creatively and well beyond the call and hours of duty throughout the negotiations. Among them were Caroline Bolger, Martin Burke, Bernard Davenport, David Donoghue, Ann Dugdale, Yvonne Elisson, Peter McIvor, Daire Ó Críodáin, Declan O'Donovan, Colm Ó Floinn, Breifne O'Reilly, Mary Qualey, Mary Shanahan and James Sharkey.

Building Westminster Commitment to the Anglo-Irish Agreement

RICHARD RYAN

In June 1982, seconded from the Department of Foreign Affairs to the European Commission in the Cabinet of Commissioner Richard Burke, I worked with Liam Hourican, Michael Lillis, Catherine Day and others. In early 1983 Michael Lillis was requested by the taoiseach, Garret FitzGerald, and the minister for foreign affairs, Peter Barry, to return to the department as head of the Anglo-Irish division. From our distance, we understood that this move was connected to urgent concerns within the government regarding the grievous situation in Northern Ireland, and its impact on the security of our state.

In June 1983 I received a call from Seán Donlon, secretary general of the DFA. He said he was requested at political level to invite me to Dublin to discuss some pressing matters that he could not go into on the phone. Two mornings later Michael Lillis and I walked on the Great South Wall to the Poolbeg lighthouse. Michael elaborated in strict confidence the taoiseach's determination to engage with Margaret Thatcher and her government on the dangers, including to the stability of our state, of the Northern Ireland situation. This decision was in full appreciation of the possibilities of failure to engage Mrs Thatcher, including the domestic threat that a repulse could pose for the Irish government. He said that, to have sufficient meaning and effect, the objectives would have to be sufficiently deep and comprehensive to achieve formal parity with the unionist majority for the nationalist minority in Northern Ireland. He listed the principal and essential areas of change required to achieve those objectives. The formidable scale of those changes was clearly such as to require major legislative support by the parliament at Westminster. He said the scale of difficulties lying in the way, from engaging the prime minister herself, with her official and personal reputation as a diehard unionist, to working with her closest political and official advisers and somehow achieving a resounding majority of the 650-member House of Commons, had been weighed. There were no illusions in this regard. It was entirely possible that the project would collapse at the first engagement between the taoiseach and the prime minister. Nevertheless, it was a settled matter for the taoiseach. Engagement was to begin shortly in informal contact at high official level, between himself and David Goodall, a deputy under-secretary seconded from the Foreign and Commonwealth Office to the Cabinet Office with responsibility for intelligence and security matters.

Michael Lillis said he was conveying a proposal that I should terminate my position in the European Commission and join the embassy in London, mandated personally with a specific set of objectives. I would shadow the necessarily confidential intergovernmental contacts and negotiations as they would hopefully develop. I would build and broaden contacts across parliament, with strong emphasis on the Conservative members, including many of those most likely to question or oppose major new cooperation on Northern Ireland with the Irish government. The essential outcome of this project had to be heightened parliamentary interest, real understanding, and the eventual commitment of a meaningful majority of their supporting votes for whatever outcome the two governments could achieve and agree to put before the two parliaments. On 1 October 1983 I took up duty at the London embassy.

The Westminster milieu was settling busily following Margaret Thatcher's massive June election victory —the Conservatives were buoyed with 397 seats, the greatest majority since Labour's in 1945, and still in hearty mood following the Falklands victory a year before. Ten days later, the triumphant party held its annual conference in Blackpool. I took the train and on arrival dropped into a pub to have a snack on the way to the conference. I saw a familiar figure standing mournfully over the buffet counter. It was Grey Gowrie. We became friends in Dublin, where he was born, in the mid-1960s. His busy life had brought him into British political circles, including Margaret Thatcher's inner circle of friends. Having most recently been Jim Prior's minister of state for Northern Ireland, he had just become minister for the arts and would become chancellor of the Duchy of Lancaster, a Cabinet post, a year later. He was returning to London and we agreed to lunch at the Carlton Club on the following Monday.

The lobby and bars of the Imperial Hotel, the conference hotel, at 7.00 p.m. were a hubbub packed with veteran and rookie MPs and spouses, constituency representatives and party members, journalists, diplomatic observers and political hangers-on. With our press officer, Pat Hennessy, I gazed around. It was like a salmon river in spate, a grouse moor on a good day. Here they were, and here we were, with clearly very few approachable political figures known to the embassy in comparison with many more easily approached journalists, now hunting busily among the crowd. It was also clear that within an hour this Conservative swarm would vanish, on their eager way to dinner engagements. Then something happened. I had noticed among the crowd a jovial, stout fellow with busy eyes and a faded Garrick Club tie, clearly of some importance, standing at the centre of a noisy, festive group. He had glanced quickly several times in our direction. He then detached himself, crossed the floor and asked me which constituency I was from. I replied that I was from the Irish embassy, here to observe the proceedings. Without blinking, 'What a good idea,' he said. 'Look here, I'm having a drinks party in about half an hour in suite 113. Would you care to join us?' I said we would be delighted, and he returned to his group. I asked my colleague who was this interesting fellow. 'That fellow,' said Pat, 'is Baron Alistair McAlpine of West Green, and of the Fusiliers. He is the treasurer of the Conservative Party and one of Mrs Thatcher's closest friends. His conference parties are famous and exclusive.'

On our arrival at Alistair McAlpine's crowded suite, he was receiving at the door and chatting with Denis Thatcher. Alistair introduced me and we were joined by another arrival, Gordon Reece, Mrs Thatcher's media guru. There were no raised eyebrows at the presence, strictly speaking, of foreign diplomatic representatives. The introductions led to surprisingly easy conversation. Shortly after, Denis Thatcher introduced me to Leon Brittan, home secretary, and Nigel Lawson, chancellor of the exchequer, neither of whom showed any surprise at being introduced to an Irish diplomat in this Tory inner sanctum. In due course, chatting with an eminent journalist, Ian Aitken of the *Guardian*, he called over Norman Tebbit, employment secretary. We had an affable conversation that initiated a tough but always frank relationship, not least following the Brighton bomb exactly a year later. Leaving at 11.00, I mentioned to Alistair that our ambassador, Noel Dorr, was arriving the following day. He asked if I would return and introduce him, which I did. Noel was welcomed, and was in turn soon engaged in meeting interesting figures. Alistair, who was soon to become a good friend, suggested that I join his nightly gathering during the conference. This invitation was renewed over the six years of my London posting. By the end of the conference, my notebook was filled with notes on many important political figures who, amazingly to me at this early stage, seemed unsurprised and open to lively conversation about many issues. It was a fair start.

Thereafter in London, targets were selected and broadened. The circle of Conservative members long on the embassy's social lists were pleasant to meet and this revealed the largely social character of their relationships over the years with successive Irish diplomats. A better way was needed to go deeper and much wider into the Tory ranks.

Before long a few strong relationships were established with carefully selected, approachable, seasoned MPs. Following initial one-to-one conversations, they proved amenable to help build a most valuable guide to very large numbers of MPs. One such was Sir Marcus Fox, member for Shipley since 1970. He was exceptionally astute and hard-headed. We met for a full day with the lists of the entire membership of the House of Commons, on which he commented, with the exception of some just-arrived members. Personal files grew with details of individual MPs' general reputations, strengths, weaknesses, possible professional prospects for political advancement, interests, disinterests, likely susceptibility to Irish diplomatic approach, likely indifference or hostility. David Crouch, member for Canterbury since 1966, also offered to share his long knowledge, following the same procedure as Marcus Fox. Another from the same mould was Sir Peter Hordern, member for Horsham since 1964. Bill Benyon, member for Buckingham from 1970, when he defeated the incumbent Robert Maxwell, and for Milton Keynes from 1983, also guided me through the lists and became an active and unstinting supporter of our project through the negotiating period and after. Peter Temple-Morris, member for Leominster, on the so-called wet side of the party and associated with Michael Heseltine, was fully on board and later played a crucial role during very delicate manoeuvrings, in the face of rapidly aroused unionist hostility, to have appointed an appropriately balanced British membership, undominated by unionist interests, of the nascent British–Irish Inter-Parliamentary Body. Sir Antony Buck, member for Colchester and later Colchester North since 1961, appointed under-secretary for defence in 1972—a kindly, colourful and troubled personality—was also a very wise and shrewd observer of the Westminster scene and a rich source of guidance to a great number of fellow members.

These, and others over time, proved hugely valuable in the process of judging how to identify and penetrate the very large right wing of the party at Westminster. Categories began to identify themselves. One category was of those whose unionist mindset and total hostility to any engagement whatever with 'Southern Ireland' verged on caricature. Enoch Powell, Julian Amery, Ivor Stanbrook and Nicholas Budgen were ripened representatives of this category. A very much larger group, also on the hard right, were those who —in the considered view of my advisers —were tough nuts to crack in the round, but also ought to be approachable, with care, on the issue. This was the key category: unequivocal Thatcher devotees, prime targets. The wisest approach that commended itself was to build as much information about them as possible, then to suggest lunch and to become acquainted.

In the light of this, they were invited, with spouses, to one of our now established weekly Tuesday evening buffet dinners at home for about 30 guests, at which they mingled with parliamentary colleagues, senior government officials, and interesting friends of ours: 'the usual suspects'. The next step, all going well, was to meet again and discuss current issues before returning to Northern Ireland-related issues. In this way, many very good working relationships and indeed friendships were nourished. At Westminster, it was pleasant to become routinely nodded through by the highly alert police officers stationed at the entrances and within Westminster, including to the chamber, the terrace, the bars and other specifically reserved areas.

Initial meetings were occasionally somewhat strained, at least to begin with. In such cases, it proved best to canter round the course of general conversation and draw on reported interests of the guest. Country pursuits like shooting were common interests; history and wine were others. Above all, they were very happy, and perhaps relieved, to delve into the hive-like goings-on at Westminster. In this way, my own comprehensions of those goings-on also grew.

The right-wing spectrum was a very wide one. Of course, personalities varied hugely. An example might be Ian Gow. In 1979 he entered Downing Street with Margaret Thatcher as parliamentary private secretary to the prime minister. He later became minister for housing, then a minister at the Treasury. I met with Grey Gowrie one day for lunch in the Garrick Club, where we ran into Gow in the bar together with a mutually friendly journalist. The wide-ranging conversation took us through to about three o'clock: White Ladies for Ian Gow and no lunch for anyone. I suggested lunch the following week and we met in the Garrick at 1.00, separating at 5.20 when he strode briskly back to Westminster. Before we parted, however, he revealed that he had sought his close friend Enoch Powell's view on lunching with me. Powell's reply, he said, was 'I'd rather have lunch with Ribbentrop!'

Ian Gow was always absolutely straight about his convictions, his thoughts and his worries. Our relationship deepened and soon included my wife and his wife, Jane. Our discussions concentrated largely on Northern Ireland issues. We travelled together to Dublin at the taoiseach's invitation. Gow expressed his concerns clearly, showing that his original suspicions about the Irish government's objectives were evaporating. He was frank about the quandary he was finding himself in, between the direction the prime minister might be taking in her discussions with Dublin and his deep sense of loyalty and obligation to his unionist friends. However, he said his contacts with our side enabled him to reassure his friends that the Irish government's objectives were focused on formal parity within Northern Ireland as an essential precursor to a successful peace process. He continued to the end, however, to worry about the impact of a Dublin–London agreement on the ground in Northern Ireland. A footnote to that visit to Dublin was my surprise at the very heavy level of close protection he received throughout. Hindsight confirms the accuracy of the perceived threat level to a brave and honest man.

An example from much further right on the political spectrum was Nick Budgen, Budgie to his friends, a cousin of Ian Gow and member for Wolverhampton South West. A gifted speaker possessed of a vicious verbal sting, and far too unreliable for promotion, he relished the cut and thrust of parliamentary life. Acclamation greeted his receiving the *Spectator* Parliamentarian of the Year award. We met for lunch at the Carlton Club. He lunged first, probing my background and interests. Then, as I turned to Northern Ireland, he cut across to say:

> Forgive me, but I feel I have to say that, as the representative of a marginal and residual race, you actually strike me as being at least three-quarters educated. Behind the pleasant crowd now in power, you have been sent over here by the culture of that gun-running gangster Hockey [*sic*] and his gun-toting friends who of course will not meet us face to face. But you may convey to them and to Garret FitzGerald and his friends that my friends and I will oppose with all our power any say whatever by the Eire government in the affairs of the United Kingdom!

He then poured scorn on Mrs Thatcher for even meeting with representatives of our government, with which he saw no need on the part of Her Majesty's government to have diplomatic relations. In subsequent meetings, over an occasional lunch, running into each other at Westminster and even—surprisingly at first—at dinner as his guest there, he became much more civil and interested in earnest conversation. As a certain conveyer of our conversations to his friends, he was also a useful channel of selective information feed. Much later, when Ian Gow was killed agonisingly by an IRA car-bomb on 30 July 1990, his private funeral, to which I was invited by Jane Gow, was also the scene of my last meeting with Budgie. He grasped both my hands, in tears, saying he had been wrong about everything and he realised now that our approach all along had been 'honourable and right'.

Ivor Stanbrook, member for Orpington, had a tall flagpole flying the Union Jack on his lawn and, in repeated skirmishes, he stood his ground to the end. Eventually, following the funeral of Sir John Biggs-Davison in 1988 at Waltham Abbey in the Epping Forest area of Essex, I joined a large number of his MP friends returning on the London train. They, led by the entreaties of Antony Buck, prodded Stanbrook to behave civilly to me as a mutual good friend of theirs and of the devoted Catholic Shire Tory we had just laid to rest. He sputtered angrily in his response that 'I will most certainly never fraternise with the fifth column agent of a hostile foreign power whose insidious purpose is to subvert the integrity of the United Kingdom. So there!', and then sat back, quivering redly on his seat.

As we passed through 1984 and into 1985 the general level of interest and the breadth of our relationships, with their greatly changing comprehension of our policies as perceived from Dublin, was having visible impact across the Commons membership. Media speculation and word of mouth indicated that Mrs Thatcher was indeed thinking about Northern Ireland and was in contact with the taoiseach. Almost daily embassy reporting was found useful in refining Dublin's perceptions of the deepening degrees of engagement by MPs across the full spectrum. There was a clear sense that Ireland was moving to the centre as an issue of serious interest to the government, therefore to parliament, and therefore, individually, to them.

Inevitably, there were spasms. One was the Brighton bomb at 2.54 a.m. on Friday, 12 October 1984, the night before the final day of the annual Conservative conference. Before dawn, in

Dublin officials gathered in the taoiseach's home with an open line to my bedroom in the hotel beside the Grand Hotel. Work began over the line on the text of a message from the taoiseach and the people of Ireland. Urgency was added when we heard of Mrs Thatcher's determination that, defying the outrage, her scheduled keynote end-of-conference morning speech would commence precisely on time.

Next morning, as the search for the dead and injured continued amid the rubble to which the centre of the hotel had been reduced, we brought the text by arrangement through the police cordons and delivered it for the prime minister's attention. A half-hour later, in her speech, Mrs Thatcher made early specific reference to the taoiseach's message and drew on the text. The statement, to a waking Britain, certainly had a crucially positive impact through the media, which cauterised to a considerable degree the IRA-intended and understandable national wave of strong public feelings at this Ireland-related outrage. Noel Dorr, who had been in Dublin the previous day, managed to arrive in Brighton in time to join our efforts to build among our many contacts on this strong message of solidarity expressed by the taoiseach. He visited Norman Tebbit, injured in hospital and awaiting news of his wife, who was severely injured and still buried in the rubble.

Another spasm occurred a month later, following the November 1984 meeting in London between the taoiseach and the prime minister. Her unscripted, ill-judged remarks containing the famous 'Out … out … out' drumbeat caused some consternation in the Irish government and in public opinion, and provoked rare unionist joy. The embassy immediately informed a selected number of well-respected Conservative MPs of the unintended damage. They in turn informed Downing Street of their concern. I was told that these messages had been well taken. A second, major upside of the incident was that the unionist MPs and their Conservative supporters judged the negotiations to be at an end. In reality, any careful reading of the public joint conclusions of the summit, perhaps obscured by the political storm that may have diverted close attention from them, revealed that the bone structure of what was a year later to be fleshed out in the form of the Anglo-Irish Agreement was there to see. This cloud cover hung helpfully over the steady resumption of the intergovernmental negotiations at the beginning of 1985.

Despite the continuing secrecy surrounding the negotiation process, growing whiffs of more informed media speculation as to serious British–Irish intergovernmental possibilities were now pre-occupying the minds of the great majority of MPs. The embassy, including its alert press section, was increasingly able to report to Dublin confidence in a powerfully positive response, should an agreed outcome emerge from the ongoing negotiations. During these weeks, a large number of well-regarded and fully engaged MPs were eager to discuss any points that they could usefully and effectively deploy in speeches should, as expected, an intergovernmental agreement require parliamentary approval preceded by a debate in the House. In response to this interest, discreet individual drafting meetings took place.

We engaged throughout with Labour members expressing serious interest in the issue. Outstanding players were Alf Dubs, Clive Soley, Roy Hattersley, Stuart Bell, George Foulkes, Clare Short, Mo Mowlam and Robin Cook. Don Concannon, shadow spokesman on Northern Ireland, was steady but busy with other interests. Kevin McNamara, member for Hull seats since 1966, and others around him resented the party's important biparti-san approach with the government on major Northern Ireland policy. A lunch with him at the September Labour conference in Bournemouth confirmed his commitment to achieve a radical policy departure, demanding British withdrawal from Northern Ireland. A lunch with the party leader, Neil Kinnock, a few days later led to Kinnock's decision, made clear to the party, that if there were to be a major Commons debate on an Anglo-Irish Agreement, he would write and deliver the Labour Party's speech. In the event, Kevin McNamara absented himself from the House for that debate, including Neil Kinnock's most brilliant speech, and the vote that followed it.

We also maintained friendly personal contact with the SDP–Liberal Alliance, and attended their conferences. They were by and large very supportive of ongoing intergovernmental discussions and were ready to give strong vocal and voting support to a positive outcome.

The intergovernmental negotiations entered their final phase in late autumn 1985. At this point a further political spasm occurred. There had long been a settled and agreed commitment in the draft agreement to the establishment of a joint secretariat within Northern Ireland, staffed by Irish and British officials, to handle daily implementation of matters arising under the agreement. I received a call from Michael Lillis: London had just informed Dublin that the secretariat's geographical presence inside Northern Ireland was off the table for security reasons. The prime minister had pronounced that she could not go against her security advisers. Amid all the checks and balances constructed with exquisite care during the protracted negotiations, this was a crucial red-line component for the Irish government, long embedded in the now virtually concluded draft text of the agreement.

The question of physical security had been assessed by both British and Irish security services. It was not amenable to renegotiation. Michael said it had been decided in Dublin that if the taoiseach were to meet Mrs Thatcher on it, it was extremely likely that she would refuse to go against the security services' advice, neither side would be prepared to back down, and the entire agreement could collapse. Therefore the taoiseach had not yet been informed of the development. It was decided that I should immediately seek a low-key meeting with Charles Powell, Mrs Thatcher's powerful private secretary and foreign policy adviser in Downing Street. I was to press as best I could for the most urgent reconsideration of the issue by the prime minister's advisers, with a view to withdrawal of the message to the taoiseach.

My request for an urgent meeting with Powell was granted immediately. While standing in the visitors' waiting room off the hall in Number 10, glancing at the old glazed bookcase with its large accumulation of favourite books placed there by many generations of outgoing prime ministers and preparing myself for the meeting, I recalled Mrs Thatcher's well-documented occasional custom of throwing open the door to this room on her way out or in. It was widely regarded as a personal way she had of showing who was in charge of the house. I had hitherto not experienced this practice, but I knew that under no circumstances could I be engaged by her on the subject of my visit.

The door opened behind me. As it could have been anybody, I felt able not to turn around immediately. Then her unmistakable voice said 'Mr Ryan?' I turned quickly and bade her good morning. She asked me what I was doing. On the back foot, I said I was just then wondering which of her predecessors could possibly have placed the collected poems of William McGonagall in the bookcase—'Balfour, perhaps?' She stared blankly for a moment. I collected myself and said I was here to see Charles. She asked what about. Knowing that she most certainly knew the answer, I said, truthfully, while scrabbling for a domestic metaphor, that it was our practice at official level between London and Dublin, following meetings and communications between herself and the taoiseach, to run over the main points covered, just to iron out any little wrinkles of possible misunderstanding on either side, and thereby to assist preparations for the next meeting. She stood unblinking for a few moments, bade me good morning with a little knowing smile, and was gone.

I heard Charles trotting down the stairs. He had a strained look. 'Did Margaret speak to you?' I said 'yes', and he asked what had been discussed. I said we had a brief word on the poetry of William MacGonagall. He looked hard at me and said, 'So you didn't discuss what I believe you are here for?' I confirmed that this was the case. He was clearly, like myself, relieved. He proposed that we sit in the Cabinet Room, 'the safest room in England'. He sat in the prime minister's chair and invited me to sit opposite, in that of the chancellor of the Exchequer. We went at it for several hours.

We finished on my slow observation that such a breakdown at this final stage on a major, previously agreed element, so clearly understood as a supporting pillar of the agreement on the Irish side, would not be understood in Washington. He saw me out. I informed Michael that Charles had of course been stern and formally implacable but that he had taken full note of my points. A few days passed, then a few more. There was no further approach by London on this issue.

Following the signature of the agreement on 15 November, the prime minister reported to the House on the 18th. During the short debate, the fury of the unionists was unbridled, most powerfully that of Ian Paisley and Enoch Powell. Paisley used the words 'treachery' and 'deceit'. John Hume and Ian Gow joined to thrust these words back at him. Roy Beggs (Antrim, East) referred to deceitful betrayal. Mrs Thatcher was now sitting quite still, her face frozen in controlled anger. The venerable David Crouch closed speeches from the floor with restrained, elegant compliments to the prime minister. Turning slowly towards the unionist cluster on their benches, he intoned pointedly, 'Let them fight their cause and argue their case. We can well hear them. This is a matter for the whole Parliament.'

Afterwards, Mrs Thatcher, clearly stung and, we heard, concerned at the massive street responses in Northern Ireland, declared that she wanted the imminent debate in the Commons before the vote on the agreement to be of the shortest possible duration, within an afternoon. I had a private meeting with a close, immensely shrewd friend, Murdo Maclean. He was a key figure on parliamentary procedure as principal private secretary to the government chief whip in Downing Street, and was always referred to in Commons debates across the dispatch box as 'the usual channels'. He was regarded by all as the man who knew everything about everything. He glanced through a list of very strong and highly respected MPs who stood ready and well prepared to support the prime minister and the government on the agreement. He listened further and agreed that, by the wide complementarity of their speeches, they would greatly broaden perceptions everywhere of the weight and determination of parliamentary support for it. He agreed also that this depth and breadth of support would easily justify a full two-day debate on it in the government's strong interest. Finally, raising his eyebrows, he was much taken by my (conservative) calculation that there would be not fewer than 460 votes in favour of the agreement and not more than 50 against, including all the unionists and diehard Conservative unionists, not least because a very large number of initially hostile Conservatives had agreed to give it a chance and support it or, at worst but very helpfully, to abstain. Murdo judged these considerations to carry persuasive weight. Deploying his unique skills and style, he passed them upwards in the Downing Street system. We heard that they had been accepted by the prime minister. A two-day debate was agreed, to take place on 26 and 27 November.

Thus the debate on the agreement in the House of Commons took place over two full days, totalling thirteen hours. Throughout, the House was filled above capacity. The sustained drama on all sides in the packed, excited House evoked Tennyson—*So all day long the noise of battle roll'd*, and it rolled again throughout the second day. It was characterised here and there by soaring oratory, Biblical flashings and thunderings, choked breast-beating, subtlety, rage, silken logic, venom, and a great deal of sound common sense.

The House divided at 10.00 p.m. on the second evening, and the result was announced. It recorded 473 votes in favour with 47 against—a majority of 426. As the MPs flowed from the chamber, there was, palpably, a feeling common to all present, whatever their judgement on it, that something of great importance had happened.

Afterwards, I was invited to a drink in Downing Street. During the conversation there, the government chief whip told me he had just heard that the government had that day received the largest majority at Westminster in the twentieth century.

Some Thoughts on the 'Travellers' and on Maryfield

DÁITHÍ O'CEALLAIGH

When the Fine Gael/Labour government was elected towards the end of 1982, it faced unprecedented problems in dealing with Northern Ireland and with the British government. The inertia of the Labour government following the collapse of the arrangements made at Sunningdale, and the stand-off between the Thatcher government and Sinn Féin over prison conditions that had led to the hunger strikes, had created a situation that the Irish government believed needed to be addressed urgently if Northern Ireland was not to descend further into chaos. The government believed the threat to the security of the Irish state was real.

There were three main aspects to Irish government policies: first, the attempt through the New Ireland Forum to redefine the meaning of Irish nationalism; second, an increased engagement with Northern Ireland designed, *inter alia*, to address the discrimination faced by the minority; and third, efforts to improve the British Irish–relationship, particularly regarding Northern Ireland. The last of these was particularly difficult, as David Goodall had explained to Michael Lillis in their walk by the Grand Canal: Thatcher and the Tory Second World War generation had a distaste and suspicion of Ireland arising from our neutrality. He also referred to the venomous comments on Ireland and the Irish in the Cabinet the day after the Provisional IRA bombing of the Horse Guards.

I want to discuss the second of these three issues. First, I want to talk about the efforts made to increase understanding of the problems faced by the minority in Northern Ireland and the increased engagement with the British designed to resolve these problems. Second, I want to say something about the Anglo-Irish secretariat established in Northern Ireland in the aftermath of the Anglo-Irish Agreement, from the point of view of both the issues dealt with and the personal difficulties faced by the staff.

THE TRAVELLERS

The new foreign minister, Peter Barry, was determined to alleviate what he called the nightmare of the northern nationalists through greater Irish government engagement in northern Ireland and with the British government. From the outbreak of the Troubles in 1969, officials of the Department of Foreign Affairs had travelled in the north, where they had engaged with a wide spectrum of politicians but especially with the SDLP. Significant among these early 'travellers' were Eamonn Gallagher, Seán Donlon and John McColgan. Under Barry, the amount of time spent by the travellers in Northern Ireland was greatly increased, as was the range of their contacts. A variety of issues, from policing and conditions in the prisons to fair employment and housing, were systematically investigated. The problems faced by the minority, whether of a specific or a generic nature, were raised regularly with the British at both official and ministerial levels with the intent of seeking to resolve them. One reason for this, as Michael Lillis has mentioned, was to underpin the position of the SDLP and to stop the slide in the minority community towards Sinn Féin arising from the hunger strikes and the political vacuum in Northern Ireland. Another was to address the alienation of many in the minority community in the north from the state institutions because of the failure of those institutions, be they British or Northern Irish, to address their grievances.

A substantial component of the alienation from British rule of the nationalist minority was the concentration of the British security efforts in Catholic areas and the impact on daily life of

84

these security impediments. Repeatedly, nationalists complained to us of harassment, of something frequently akin to humiliation in vehicle and personal stoppages and questioning, especially by the UDR, and of their sense that security policy was discriminatory and sectarian. Obviously, this came on top of a 50-year history in Northern Ireland of political, economic and social discrimination, which had already prompted an extensive disaffection from British/unionist rule. Tactless security efforts were driving people towards Sinn Féin and the Provisional IRA.

I returned in summer 1982 from the embassy in London, where I had worked on the press and political side since 1977. I served in the Anglo-Irish division and worked as a traveller from the end of 1982 until December 1985, when I joined the Anglo-Irish secretariat as deputy to Michael Lillis. I remained in Maryfield, where we were based, until I departed for New York in the summer of 1987.

On the political side, John Hume had always maintained close contact with the Irish government at both political and official levels. There was contact from time to time with other SDLP politicians. These contacts were widened to include frequent meetings with the SDLP deputy leader, Seamus Mallon, and with other SDLP figures including Bríd Rogers, Eddie McGrady, Paddy O'Donoghue, Austin Currie, Joe Hendron, Paddy O'Hanlon and many others, both to gain a better understanding of local problems and to brief them on the thinking of the government as it evolved. Alliance leaders, especially John Cushnahan, were also met with frequently, as were some unionist politicians, including a bit later at least two members of the DUP.

On the religious side, regular meetings were held with Cardinal Ó Fiaich, Archbishop Cathal Daly, Bishop Eddie Daly in Derry and numerous catholic clergy, particularly those such as Father Denis Faul and Father Raymond Murray who had concerns about human rights, the behaviour of the security forces and conditions in the prisons. Close and frequent contact was maintained with the prison chaplains. Numerous meetings were held with Church of Ireland clergy, including the Archbishop of Armagh, Dr Robin Eames, who had good relations with the unionist leaders. A wide group of Presbyterian ministers and other Protestant clergy, including Methodists and Quakers, were regularly visited.

Systematic contact was made with several important figures in the legal profession, especially with those involved in criminal trials, including P.J. McGrory and Christopher Hill, whose insights into the criminal justice system provided us with much to think about. The media were also cultivated, both to give us a better idea of conditions in Northern Ireland and to enable us to inform them of Irish government thinking as it progressed. People involved in education, public housing and fair employment, as well as trade unionists, kept us informed. A wide range of people in civic society or involved in voluntary agencies were contacted, as were some relatives of victims. In effect we sought views from practically every corner of society except from those involved in paramilitary activity.

As time passed, the government built up a much better picture of conditions in Northern Ireland. The information helped inform the government in its approach to the New Ireland Forum and particularly in the negotiations with the British government that led to the Anglo-Irish Agreement. Specific incidents raised with us in Northern Ireland might be raised at official level with the British embassy in Dublin, or occasionally in ministerial meetings between Barry and the secretary of state for Northern Ireland. On other occasions distinct patterns of discrimination or misbehaviour might be raised. The most serious issues were raised by Garret FitzGerald with Margaret Thatcher.

This intense involvement in Northern Ireland, seeking to remedy minority grievances through engagement with the British government, represented a distinct change in Irish government policy and was a particular interest of Peter Barry, who was largely responsible for it. Michael Lillis had developed a system whereby various reports, whether they came from the embassy in London, from the travellers in Northern Ireland or wherever, were circulated on a weekly basis to a select number of people in the Cabinet and in other government departments, thus informing a wider circle of the issues.

The information-gathering and relationship-building of the travellers helped the government in Dublin to establish, on solid and informed grounds, its reach in Anglo-Irish negotiations— what would fly, what would not. The acceptance of the union, in my view, came from the reality of its immutability/intractability reflected continually in their reports. Equally, the repeated recitation of unaddressed nationalist grievances essentially helped to shape the sought-after role of Dublin in pitching itself as the representative of nationalists on those issues. Overall the traveller role was unique in being much more than intelligence-gathering: it involved relationship-building, being open and being welcomed (if quietly on the unionist side) by representatives of both communities. Also bear in mind the solid and abiding consensus during the period 1982–7 across government members in Dublin on Northern Ireland, forged by both a common reading of the reports from there and a steady stream of government memos shaped by the travellers' information flow.

The traveller reports brought attention to Northern Ireland that in its detail was very new. Let me just mention what I think are a couple of generalised results of this policy. First, I think more people in the north, including those like Father Faul who previously had doubts about the sincerity of Irish governments, began to believe that the Irish government was serious about trying to address their problems. Consequently, an increasing number of people in Northern Ireland began to trust the Irish government. Second, most areas of concern identified over the preceding three years were enumerated in the Anglo-Irish Agreement. After the agreement many of these issues were dealt with in a much more effective way than previously, because the Anglo-Irish conference and the Maryfield secretariat provided a mechanism to do so. The British were now under a formal obligation, set in international law (the treaty was registered with the UN), to seek resolution to differences between the two governments.

A final comment on travellers is that they were at times putting themselves in harm's way. It is a matter of some luck that none were injured or assassinated; many of them, including myself, can remember times when we felt seriously at risk.

THE ANGLO-IRISH SECRETARIAT

I intend first to say something about life in the Anglo-Irish Secretariat and then something about the work undertaken there.

The secretariat, located in a converted office building called Maryfield in Holywood, just outside Belfast, was made up of Irish and British civil servants. Michael Lillis was in charge on the Irish side while I was the deputy. The late Noel Ryan, an assistant secretary from the Department of Justice, looked after cooperation with the British on security matters. Security cooperation was an important British priority for the Anglo-Irish Agreement, a priority shared by Dublin. Other Dublin officials included the late Padraic Collins, Daire O'Criodain, Pat Scullion and Tom Bolster. Our secretaries were Caroline Bolger, Mary Qualey, Frances Killilea and Mary Shanahan. We had one non-civil servant who was our cook, Barry Noonan. The British worked office hours while the Irish worked on a five-day shift, replaced by a weekend crew. Later the more junior Irish staff worked a week on and a week off. Most of the surviving members of the Irish team were interviewed in University College, Dublin in 2015 and that evidence has been published. It is available at http://www.drb.ie/essays/bunker-days.

Maryfield had been constructed in the 1960s by Wimpey as a headquarters when they were building the M1 motorway. It was in the shape of a T, and had two storeys: the top storey was the living and working quarters for the Irish side; the British area and the dining and kitchen facilities for the Irish were on the ground floor. Before our arrival the windows had been made bulletproof, but there were no curtains on the windows. We were not allowed out of the building at first and RUC men patrolled continuously 24-hours a day around the building, armed with submachine guns. The living conditions were exceedingly primitive until Secretary of State for Northern Ireland Tom King visited a few months after our establishment. He was horrified and had many improvements made.

A reflection of the security threat is that we were all obliged to make our wills. The gardaí made sure that there were means of identifying us if something untoward happened. We initially travelled in military aircraft, with the Aer Corps from Baldonnel to Aldergrove military airport and from there to Maryfield in British army helicopters, later in RUC vehicles. Much later we travelled with the RUC from the border. Two of our families, Michael's and mine, were under 24-hour police protection in Dublin.

One of my abiding memories is going in on the initial flight on 8 December 1985; it was a historic moment. We represented the presence, for the first time since partition in 1921, of the Irish government within Northern Ireland, within the United Kingdom to deal with Northern Ireland affairs: it was unique. We, the representatives of the Irish government, were engaged with the British government in how Northern Ireland should be governed. On the other hand, I was actually quite scared. Maryfield was between an RUC vehicle repair shop on which there was a big flag saying 'Ulster Says No' and Palace Barracks. But Palace Barracks wasn't only a British army barracks; it was the headquarters of the UDR. We had the advantage of sharing a common entrance with the RUC depot from which there was constant coming and going, which made it impossible for those who were picketing the entrance to differentiate between the vehicles, especially since those we travelled in belonged to either the RUC or the Northern Ireland Office. There was a constant protest at the entrance until eventually the last protester, George Seawright, abandoned his caravan to the elements.

Michael and I were the only Irish civil servants inside Maryfield in January 1986 when it was attacked by about 18,000 unionists who had marched from Derry. We were quite frightened, because we were afraid that, if the demonstrators pushed the RUC aside and pushed us out of the building, we'd be forced into the hands of the UDR in Palace Barracks behind us, and while we had a certain trust in the RUC, we had very little trust in the UDR. It was pouring rain, literally sheets of rain driving almost horizontally across the field between us and the demonstrators. The RUC man in charge came in every twenty minutes, and when we asked how matters were, he'd say: 'See that rain? It's worth a battalion of soldiers.' As contemporary photographs attest, many policemen were injured protecting us that day. The RUC were exceedingly good at looking after us. We were very well staffed by our secretarial staff, by our cook, who travelled up with us from Dublin, and by the local staff, including drivers, kitchen and cleaning staff, who took considerable risk at a time of great tension.

The issues that were raised by the secretariat, especially in the early days, were based on those enumerated in the Anglo-Irish Agreement. Some were resolved within the secretariat; others went to the Anglo-Irish ministerial conference, which met almost monthly, chaired by Peter Barry and Tom King, with other ministers present depending on the topic and generally also with the presence of the police chiefs. The conference was serviced by the secretariat.

Initially the NIO was utterly unresponsive on issues that we raised in the secretariat. Because of this we proposed the introduction of a joint log to record topics or incidents raised by either side and to track responses on a regular and frequent basis. Only when confronted by the log and its implicit and threatening implication that, unless they responded on issues, they were risking being seen as in breach of the Anglo-Irish Agreement and international law did the NIO begin to respond. This gave practical substance to the agreement's 'determined efforts to resolve differences'. A related point is that the Irish side of the secretariat, thanks to the travellers, was frequently much better informed than the British side.

Within six or seven weeks, by the end of January 1986, about 40 different issues had been formally raised and logged by the Irish side, including specific incidents and general policies. Specific incidents included alleged UDR harassment, prison sentence review, a request from a person who had been arrested and wanted his belongings returned to him by the RUC, and a shooting involving two UDR soldiers (who were immediately suspended from operational duties pending an inquiry).

More generally we requested that new British army replacement regiments be properly briefed, especially about cross-border incursions. A threat assessment of cross-border terrorism was initiated at the request of the British. Cross-border road closures, the renewal of the Emergency Provisions Act, and the Flags and Emblems Act were raised in early January in preparation for a meeting of the conference. Other issues raised early on included the use of the Irish language in Northern Ireland, which led to changed regulations. On 6 January 1986 we submitted a paper on public appointments so that we would have an influence on appointments to public bodies. By mid-January papers on the Newry–Dundalk road, the life sentence review board, police complaints, Northern Ireland electoral matters and a code of conduct for police had been given to the British. All of these initiatives led to important changes in the governance of Northern Ireland.

On 16 January, we raised an interesting issue in response to a request from Cardinal Ó Fiaich. Quarrying was being carried out close to Navan Fort/Emain Macha, which was an important archaeological site. In Ó Fiaich's view, the quarrying was causing severe damage to the site. Complaints had been made to the local authorities and to the Northern Ireland civil service, who had allowed the quarrying to continue. It took four or five months of very difficult negotiations—including Michael waxing eloquently over dinner to the responsible minister, Richard Needham, about the Táin Bó Cúailnge, and the importance of Navan Fort in that epic—to resolve the matter. We gave Needham Thomas Kinsella's translation of the epic; he personally overrode the Northern Ireland civil service and stopped the quarrying.

Another issue raised, in March 1986, was Divis Flats. We eventually persuaded the authorities to demolish three blocks of flats, including the Divis complex in Belfast and the Rossville complex in Derry.

The Irish side in the secretariat dealt with the Northern Ireland Office when discussing matters reserved to the British government. This related particularly to the treatment of the minority community by the security forces and by the justice system as well as other matters such as human rights that were not included in those that might be devolved. We dealt with the Northern Ireland civil service on matters that might be devolved in the event of devolution. We provided an opportunity for Irish government departments to work with their opposite numbers in the north on matters such as health, education and fair employment, to the benefit of communities on both sides of the border. These joint meetings took place in the secretariat.

A difficult issue dealt with by the secretariat was cooperation on security. For Mrs Thatcher, but also for the Irish government, improved security cooperation was an important component in the Anglo-Irish Agreement. The Department of Justice had assigned a senior and very able assistant secretary, Noel Ryan, to the secretariat to deal with the difficult, and delicate, task of handling the entire agenda of security cooperation at a time of renewed IRA and loyalist violence. Noel managed this with great professionalism, while insisting on respect for human rights and for the overall political priorities of the agreement. Regular meetings on security began to be held in the secretariat, which frequently included Jack

Hermon, the RUC chief constable, and Larry Wren, the Garda Commissioner. Jack Hermon himself came in for dinner from time to time, and later in the process the GOC Northern Ireland, who headed up the British army in Northern Ireland, would also join us for dinner.

The vast bulk of the issues raised by us were resolved satisfactorily. Our work led to changes on the ground that made a real difference to the lives of the minority community. The conduct of the UDR changed over time. Initially when harassment or other complaints were raised against the UDR there was resistance/denial/dismissal of the secretariat's complaint. Later the soldier concerned was reported as having been carpeted; later again he might be reported as fined and finally reported as dismissed. The secretariat played an important role in addressing harassment cases. This was the first time in the history of the Troubles that the security forces were held to account.

The other side, whether the NIO, the police or the Northern Ireland civil service, began to realise that we weren't trying to replace them, but were trying to help them manage Northern Ireland in a better way. We began to get a more positive response as we went along. I'm not saying from everywhere, and I'm not saying from everyone, but there were people on the other side, including people in the prison service, who sought our advice. The head of the Northern Ireland civil service, Sir Kenneth Bloomfield, who was very unhappy that he had been excluded from the negotiations of the Anglo-Irish Agreement, appointed a senior civil servant in the central secretariat, which was a sort of a cabinet office, who became a very helpful liaison between the secretariat and the Northern Ireland civil service. And he was exceedingly helpful.

The Anglo-Irish Agreement was not without risk for the Irish government. Would the minority in Northern Ireland trust the government to raise issues of concern to them; would the government, especially ministers in the joint conference, and we in the secretariat be able to convince the British and Northern Irish side of the legitimacy of those concerns; and would they be prepared to make the changes necessary to deal with those concerns? In the event the answer was yes. The agreement worked and in time led to further changes.

Finally, the House of Commons vote on the Anglo-Irish Agreement on 27 November 1985 yielded the largest majority in Thatcher's parliamentary career—473 in favour, only 47 against. This surely demonstrated to unionists that, after 64 years of engagement in Westminster, they had in reality virtually no parliamentary allies. On that basis, and even allowing for the fact that it took well over ten years for it to happen, it is reasonable to argue that the agreement and the work of Maryfield forced a major unionist rethink of their position. Also, in contrast to Harold Wilson and Labour after Sunningdale, Thatcher was resolute in the face of huge unionist demonstrations, and presumably the futility of their efforts and inability to close or even suspend Maryfield were elements in their eventual abandonment of a hard-line position.

Panel 2 Overview

MARGARET O'CALLAGHAN

The Sunningdale Agreement, the Anglo-Irish Agreement and the Good Friday Agreement are seen as a policy continuum by Irish senior civil servants, by political analysts and by historians who write about that period. One of the clearest things that emerged from this day of discussion was what Ted Smyth referred to as disparities in perception of the so-called problem of Northern Ireland on the part of politicians and civil servants on the British and Irish sides. With the exception of a key actor, Robert Armstrong, whose office and role straddled Sunningdale and the Anglo-Irish Agreement, it seems clear that over the years from Sunningdale in 1973 to the Good Friday Agreement in 1998 there is far less continuity in perception, construction and understanding of core issues in relation to Northern Ireland on the British side. Each initiative seems for British politicians and officials a new beginning.

Before Sunningdale and again before the Anglo-Irish Agreement, all the running for a political initiative on Northern Ireland was made by the Irish government. For centuries Irish issues made it onto the Westminster–Whitehall agenda only by force, persuasion or propaganda drives. The instinct to ignore Ireland runs deep in Westminster and Whitehall high-political culture

Unionist and loyalist opposition to Sunningdale was not something that the new Labour government of 1974 had been prepared to manage; obliged to deal with a discontented nationalist population and the IRA, they were not prepared to have both so-called communities against them. Therefore unionism had to be placated. Clearly up to 1975 other arms of government had been prepared, much to the Dublin government's disgust, to talk directly to the then-southern leadership of the Provisional movement.

After Sunningdale the policies of Ulsterisation, criminalisation and normalisation constituted the repertoire of British government management of Northern Ireland, reformulating the Northern Ireland problem as one of ordinary crime in an ordinary society; the Gardiner report recommended ending internment, ostensibly normalising the law and pulling back British troops to be replaced by local security forces. As the conflict shrank into the theatre of the prisons, the propaganda possibilities for the militarily challenged IRA improved. This was what Irish governments most feared in the 1980s—continuing stalemate, the radicalisation of the nationalist population on the issue of the hunger strikes, and gains for the new northern-run Sinn Féin at the ballot box.

Michael Lillis's compelling chapter shows that the Irish team assembled so astutely by Garret FitzGerald engaged London officials through the Thatcher government's preoccupations with security. A useful legacy of the Haughey era, the coordinating body of the intergovernmental council, provided the stage for the first useful discussions between David Goodall and Lillis, which Goodall spoke about so intriguingly—walking along the Grand Canal after lunch in the Grey Door was the stage. Political cooperation and questions of identity did not interest London. Lillis's gripping chapter reveals that personality, wit, charm, personal relationships, developing camaraderie, trust, affection, and shared purposes could develop once a baseline had been established. I was interested in the fact that the baseline offered by Dublin in this Goodall conversation was security cooperation, and the compelling point for Goodall was that threats to London also represented threats to the security of 'our state'. It is fascinating that this point needed to be made.

What Lillis shows is that though Charles Haughey had an innovative approach in his teapot/NATO initiative of 1980, its potential had been ended by the overplaying of the 'totality of relationships card' and the Falkland Islands imbroglio. It may however have upped the game for subsequent Irish governments. So the Lillis–Goodall canal walk clearly sought to begin a new chapter. From an Irish point of view, Sunningdale functioned as both a template and a warning: a template for power-sharing and for a London–Dublin axis; a warning in that assemblies could be brought down and London–Dublin relations could fluctuate and freeze.

Stabilising a new architecture through the three strands was the most radically innovative structural aspect of the Anglo-Irish Agreement. Designed not to be collapsible, it structurally pushed towards a power-sharing government in Northern Ireland through the mechanism of indicating deeper Irish state involvement as the alternative. Labelled by some a form of coercive consociational-ism, it certainly moved politics on. Ideologically the incorporation of the language of the New Ireland Forum and aspects of John Hume's language, and the deployment of Irish officials on the ground to speak for northern nationalists, represented the most radical intervention in Northern Ireland by the Irish state since par-tition. The 1985 agreement was the most significant event between London and Dublin on partition since 1925 and the Boundary Commission Agreement. It delivered on a wide range of reforms in Northern Ireland, whereby the Irish government on the ground through the secretariat at Maryfield monitored the treatment of northern nationalists. It gave the Irish government, whose written constitution claimed Northern Ireland to be part of its sovereign territory through articles 2 and 3, a real role in all matters except foreign policy and external defence, as well as an actual presence on the ground.

Amazingly, the Anglo-Irish Agreement garnered a phenomenally high level of support among both Tory and Labour MPs, largely due to the remarkable diplomatic gift for conversation, communi-cation, empathy and imagination of Richard Ryan. Ryan's stories of his extraordinary range of conversations with an array of Tory MPs is a historically fascinating insight into the mentality and worldviews of some remarkable individuals. Documented as they are in the Department of Foreign Affairs archives, they are anthro-pologically fascinating. This session gave a tantalising insight into the wealth of material in the archives, and perhaps other material that Richard Ryan is currently writing.

For me, Dáithí O'Ceallaigh's delineation of his role and that of the other so-called travellers in talking to and forming relationships with whole sections of nationalist opinion in the north was fascinating. This story is less well known than some other aspects of the process and deserves to be examined in greater detail, as it provides a wealth of information on the nationalist north in key periods. Do any such contacts exist today? Maryfield, as the concrete manifestation of the role of the Irish government on the ground after 1985, is a fascinating story and both Michael Lillis and O'Ceallaigh made that period, which is badly covered in academic studies, riveting. Accounts by Lillis published elsewhere reveal complementary material. I did not know that meetings took place in a variety of country houses, that there were 36 sessions, that many went on for two or three days. These three diplomats—Lillis, O'Ceallaigh and Ryan— have given us a fuller account of important events than we have been given by any previous senior Irish civil servants. They should be encouraged to keep writing and talking; this is the material we need to know now, and needs to be on the record for posterity. But there is more to be told here—that was my main conclusion at the end of our session.

Brilliant and creative civil servants change societies. I think the Anglo-Irish Agreement is the core text of this trilogy (Sunningdale, Anglo-Irish Agreement and Good Friday Agreement). It may also be the only one for which we have so full and informative an account by key participants. Ronan Fanning, key friend and adviser of both Garret FitzGerald and Lillis, and one of the only Irish analysts privy to much of this information at the time, provides in his journalistic rather than his historical writings a further gloss on this period.

The Anglo-Irish Agreement changed the dynamics of politics within Northern Ireland and between Britain and Ireland. If one wants to know why successive Irish governments were right to constantly press for some political initiative, and why the brilliant, creative, first-class work of Lillis, O'Ceallaigh and Ryan matters so much, read *Milkman* by Anna Burns. Set in 1972, it shows just what Belfast was like. Politics and diplomacy matter.

Road to Agreement:
Early 1990s and the
Downing Street Declaration

—

The Early Phase of the Irish Peace Process: The Path to the Downing Street Declaration and the First Ceasefires

MARTIN MANSERGH

The achievement of a sustainable peace in Northern Ireland required an immense and cumulative effort by innumerable people that had nonetheless to be negotiated and sealed at political level. Much groundwork had to be done, and many avenues attempted, before peace was arrived at.

The Irish government from the early 1970s, and constitutional nationalism in Northern Ireland, had in-depth support from dedicated, courageous and talented civil servants in the Anglo-Irish division of the Department of Foreign Affairs and key embassies abroad, complemented by counterparts in the taoiseach's office, the Department of Justice, and the attorney general's office. They gathered information, participated in discussions with parties, civil society and the British and American governments, and helped to inform and distil positions that might assist the twin goals of peace and a just and balanced political settlement. Travelling or working in Northern Ireland sometimes involved significant personal risk.

Governments and civil servants were united in the conviction that a solution could not be attained through violence, and that it had to be achieved, however impossible this seemed at times, by peaceful and democratic means. Realistically, any solution would not involve early achievement of the traditional national aim of a united Ireland, but nor need that aim be precluded as an option in the longer term.

The Anglo-Irish Agreement of 1985, which above all was shaped by British and Irish civil servants, was instrumental in leading to an eventual break in the prolonged political and military deadlock, even if in its immediate aftermath the opposite seemed to be the case. The agreement broke the unionist veto on political development or progress by recognising formally the right of the Irish government to make an input into British government decision-making in Northern Ireland, particularly in circumstances of continued direct rule. It gave the SDLP access to decision-making through a joint intergovernmental secretariat, enabling that party to check the electoral advance of Sinn Féin, so long as the latter was operating under and advocating a dual 'Armalite and ballot box' political strategy. Thanks to the agreement, a situation much feared by the Irish government at the time never arose, whereby electoral legitimacy might be claimed for the ongoing Provisional IRA campaign should Sinn Féin win majority support from northern nationalists.

The Anglo-Irish Agreement was intended to provide an incentive for unionists to embrace power-sharing, but it was to be a number of years before talks got under way and even then they were broken off after a couple of years without reaching an agreement. John Hume was more ambitious, wanting to bring about an end to the conflict, not just a restoration of power-sharing devolution. The republican movement, its political advance checked, could no longer be entirely confident in the efficacy of its own paramilitary veto on political progress from which it was excluded. It began tentatively, using intermediaries, to explore whether there might be purely political alternatives.

Given the degree to which any association or contact by democrats with the IRA or its surrogates was rejected, the discreet role of the Catholic Church or, more strictly speaking, of well-placed individuals within it was essential if any contact with a view to peace was to be established. Many clergy well understood that Northern Ireland was not suffering from a want of eloquent and passionate sermons denouncing violence from the pulpit. After all, the Provisional IRA had proved impervious to the pleas in Drogheda of Pope John Paul II in 1979.

Fr Alec Reid C.Ss.R., based in the Redemptorist monastery in Belfast, had for many years been engaged in local peace and mediation work and trying to prevent on the ground murderous feuds and attacks, but now wanted to enlarge his mission. From 1986 on, he made an approach to political leaders with the blessing of Cardinal Ó Fiaich. He first met Charles Haughey, then leader of Fianna Fáil in opposition, in August 1986. Fr Reid supported the case for dialogue on principles that would address the causes of conflict, rather than underwrite maximalist republican claims, by means of lengthily argued papers and proposals designed to provide a basis for the abandonment of conflict by the IRA in circumstances other than defeat. He shuttled between John Hume and Gerry Adams, also taking soundings from leading Northern Ireland Office civil servants.

Charles Haughey had returned as taoiseach in March 1987, but as head of a minority government was kept in office by the main opposition party, Fine Gael. He was duty-bound to work the Anglo-Irish Agreement, which had been registered with the UN as an international agreement, despite his earlier opposition to it, and his government did so.

Once that was established and accepted, he was still interested in exploring other avenues for progress. This included on the one hand attempts to engage the leader of the Ulster Unionist Party, James Molyneaux, in dialogue, and on the other hand assessing the willingness of the republican movement to explore a political alternative to the IRA campaign. The difficulty with the first was that Enoch Powell was Molyneaux's mentor and gatekeeper, and the leak of the possibility of an encounter would be enough to frighten the horses. The difficulty with the second avenue of advance was that it was politically high-risk, both because of the baggage that came with the arms trial of 1970 and because of the orthodoxy in the republic, championed over a long period by Garret FitzGerald, especially vis-à-vis the British, that there should be no talking to terrorists on the grounds that it gave them encouragement.

The events leading up to the establishment of the first triangular dialogue involving Sinn Féin in 1988 are set out in considerable detail in Ed Moloney's *A secret history of the IRA* (2002). One branch of it was a public dialogue that was mainly an ideological debate between the SDLP and Sinn Féin, which lasted a few months during a turbulent period of the conflict before being brought to an end without a conclusion. In secret support of this, a low-level delegation that explicitly represented Fianna Fáil rather than the government was sent by Charles Haughey, at the request of and in liaison with Fr Reid, to meet a Sinn Féin delegation in the Redemptorist monastery in Dundalk. The Fianna Fáil delegation consisted of a newly elected TD for Co. Louth, Dermot Ahern, later minister for foreign affairs, then justice; a party office-holder from Co. Meath, Richie Healy; and the taoiseach's special adviser, myself: the only one of the three at the time to wear both a party and a government hat. The Sinn Féin delegation consisted of Gerry Adams, Mitchel McLaughlin and Pat Doherty.

The special adviser is a flexible and disposable instrument in the Irish government system. He or she is a hybrid: a political civil servant, not required to be neutral, and strictly temporary—attached in terms of tenure to the office-holder. An effective adviser is nearly invisible, and keeps the head down. An elected politician's job in contrast is to be publicly visible and keep the head up, which is why it is against nature to expect a politician to be engaged in and remain silent about ultra-secret work, which may be destined to remain that way a long time. An adviser has no security of tenure and, if a cause of political embarrassment or crisis, can be required to resign or be dismissed at a moment's notice. Such things have happened over a weekend. That is far more difficult to do in the case of a permanent civil servant, who has security of tenure, but who also operates within a framework of law and administrative rules and is less free to operate at political behest on a freelance basis, and for whose actions the political office-holder is accountable to the Dáil.

There is much greater scope for deniability in the actions and operations of a special adviser, as their responsibilities are largely indeterminate and fluid. In this particular instance, the person employed—myself—had an advantage for Charles Haughey in terms of background and tradition of being far more removed from easy or credible public characterisation as a closet IRA sympathiser, dependability and also discretion being important. In the event, complete confidentiality was maintained for as long as it mattered, till past the far more sensational revelation in late November 1993 of the secret channel between the British government and the IRA that had become operational again since Margaret Thatcher's time in 1990, despite John Major's avowed disgust at the notion.

The few meetings Fianna Fáil was involved in during 1988 were essentially introductory and exploratory with no formal agenda or papers. At the outset, conflicting positions were set out with regard to the use of violence and its unacceptability to the Irish public on the one hand, and its role as a default setting on the other, with it being argued that if there were British troops in Dundalk the population would hit back. Assurances were given that there was no intention of attacking the state, but there was considerable alienation from Dublin. Republicans needed to be convinced that the British did not have an intrinsic interest in staying in Ireland, especially strategic. They would have learnt from Fr Reid's contacts with British civil servants that there was the potential for some move on this.

Scepticism was expressed from the Fianna Fáil side about the alleged neutrality of the British government with regard to the future of Northern Ireland following the Anglo-Irish Agreement. One had to distinguish between the rules of the game, which might indeed be neutral, and the desired outcome. The principal rule was the consent of a majority. There was positive stress on the potential for cooperation between nationalists, in the north, between north and south, and in Irish-America, once violence—the main cause of division between them—was removed. Historically, it was pointed out, powerful progress had been made when different strands of Irish nationalism united behind a joint strategy, as for example in the 'New Departure' agreed between Parnell, Davitt and Devoy, uniting constitutionalists, land leaguers and part of the Fenian leadership in 1878–9, which led to major breakthroughs on land reform and home rule in the 1880s as well as a disciplined and effective Irish Parliamentary Party at Westminster.

In the course of this dialogue, appreciation was expressed on the side of the republican movement of the taoiseach's speeches in America, including his support for the MacBride principles—a code of conduct relating to fair employment that should apply to US companies doing business in Northern Ireland—being adopted in many US state legislatures, as well as his stance on the Falklands during his earlier 1982 administration. The point is worth making that positions perceived by other parties, much of the media and British politicians, diplomats and civil servants as unnecessarily hard-line republican, confrontational, and 'unhelpful'—if not deeply damaging—to Anglo-Irish relations conveyed to the republican movement leadership that, in the absence of IRA violence, there was potential for a far broader swathe of nationalism to be more on the same political wavelength.

It soon became clear that the SDLP/Sinn Féin dialogue was not going anywhere beyond the setting out of their differences and that it was going to be wound up. Continuing much longer in those circumstances the supporting but secret direct dialogue between Fianna Fáil and the republican movement, in the absence of any visible timeline for a peaceful transformation of the situation, would have involved an unacceptable political risk of eventual disclosure. At that point, the assessment was that, while Adams might like to move to a more political strategy, nothing was going to happen in the near future. Violence was reassuring to many people in the ghettos, as a way of getting their own back. The suspicion was that the leadership of the republican movement wanted to run a stiffening pan-nationalist strategy alongside a continuing level of violence.

The line of contact was not abandoned, however, but maintained indirectly for a fallow three-year period through regular one-to-one meetings with Fr Reid, who persevered in his mission and was indefatigable in drawing up position papers, including a rather prolix draft of a joint statement of principles between taoiseach and British prime minister heavily weighted towards the republican perspective. Undoubtedly reflective of his dialogue with republicans as well as others, the accent was shifted from British withdrawal and unity to acceptance by the British of an unimpeded Irish right to self-determination.

In the period between 1988 and 1991, there were important changes in the backdrop. There were no prospects of a security resolution on any side, which created cumulative pressure on all sides for some other avenue to be found. Six years after the Anglo-Irish Agreement, political talks known as the Brooke–Mayhew talks had resumed, with the Irish government involved in the north–south Strand 2 and the east–west Strand 3, but not the internal Strand 1. The republican movement would have been aware of a risk, albeit not very high, that a settlement might be reached without their involvement and from which they would be excluded. A new Northern Ireland Secretary—Peter Brooke, a Tory grandee with some Irish roots—made two all-important statements: one holding out the prospect at some stage of talks with previously militant groups using colonial analogies, and a key affirmation that Britain had no selfish strategic or economic interest (independent of the will of the people of Northern Ireland) for remaining there, as might have been the case in the immediate aftermath of the Second World War.

Behind the scenes, a channel of communication last active at the time of the hunger strikes between a representative of the British security services and Martin McGuinness, facilitated by Derry-based intermediaries, was reopened, in which mutual intentions were explored in the event of a cessation of violence. Before this had progressed very far, Mrs Thatcher was replaced by John Major as prime minister. Meanwhile, the whole world scene was being transformed with the ending of apartheid in South Africa, the fall of the Berlin Wall and the reunification of Germany, and the ending of the division of Europe with the collapse of the Soviet Union. All of a sudden, problems hitherto regarded as intractable were on their way to being solved, assisted by the ending of Cold War ideological confrontation. The term 'peace process' entered the political vocabulary, initially relating to South Africa, then Northern Ireland, and subsequently to attempts to defuse multiple conflict situations around the world.

In early October 1991 the SDLP leader John Hume brought with him to a meeting with the taoiseach Charles Haughey a short first draft of a joint declaration between taoiseach and prime minister, which had a particular emphasis on the role of Europe in providing a framework for the peaceful resolution of the Northern Ireland problem. As work began on elaborating this draft, with versions and comments being passed backwards and forwards via Fr Reid,

Haughey briefed the British prime minister in general terms on this on Major's first visit to the taoiseach's new office in Government Buildings in December 1991, with more detail being supplied at official level. As Haughey left office early in the New Year, he passed the threads to his successor, Albert Reynolds.

The political imperative of peace was at the top of Albert Reynolds's agenda. He looked forward to working with John Major, whom he had first befriended when they were both EC finance ministers. He was also quickly able to establish a rapport with US president Bill Clinton, who was prepared to become involved far more deeply than any of his predecessors. The essence was to find a formula for peace that respected the fundamental positions of each of the protagonists to the conflict. The possibilities were bound by the acceptance on the part of both governments of the principle of consent as set out in the Anglo-Irish Agreement. Subject to that, there was a democratic path to Irish unity by peaceful persuasion not blocked by any British strategic or economic interest distinct from the will of the people of Northern Ireland. One of the more difficult challenges was to gain reluctant republican acceptance that exercise of the right of self-determination, as in any long-partitioned country, could only take effect if there were a concurrent majority in both parts.

For about eighteen months, a joint declaration of principles was worked up, during which time in the autumn of 1992 the taoiseach accepted that for this project to progress any further direct back-channel contact needed to be resumed. This time, Martin McGuinness was the chief interlocutor with the taoiseach's adviser. McGuinness always had one colleague with him, while Fr Reid acted as a neutral witness. The meetings at about six-week intervals took place, usually over evening tea, mostly in the first-floor recreation room of the Redemptorist monastery in Dundalk. The meetings were not solely about text, but began with discussion of the general political environment because they were also about confidence-building. They often also involved giving and receiving written transmissions.

Many of the successive early draft texts of the declaration were published in Eamonn Mallie and David McKittrick's *The fight for peace: the secret story of the Irish peace process* in 1996. When the process had gone as far as it could, Reynolds was anxious to transmit the text to London, fully realising that it was liable to be greatly altered if any agreed joint declaration were actually to emerge. As a result of mixed messages, however, even this initial handover occurred without the explicit consent of the republican movement, in effect terminating its commitment to the text. Soon afterwards, it emerged publicly that John Hume and Gerry Adams had been meeting, and they issued three statements of their own, parallel to, complementary with, but in different language from the draft joint declaration.

For a considerable period, London in discussion at the level of senior British and Irish civil servants took an interest in, but declined to engage with, what they considered to be a far too one-sided approach to peace. Arising from this, Dublin began to amend the text unilaterally without further input from or contact with Sinn Féin, though Fr Reid was kept generally informed. Since Downing Street was unwilling to proceed without at least tacit unionist consent, the draft was considerably enlarged. It took on text supplied by Archbishop Eames of Armagh, who knew the mind of unionists as well as being a confidant of James Molyneaux and a sounding-board for John Major, but also principles drafted by the Presbyterian Rev. Roy Magee, who had audience with the Combined Loyalist Military Command.

In the autumn of 1993 tensions were rising sharply in Northern Ireland, with the revelation that Hume–Adams proposals had been put to the British government (in fact, the paper handed over by Reynolds to Cabinet Secretary Robin Butler the previous June at Baldonnel airport). The British government, ostensibly preoccupied with working with the Irish government to put together a framework document for renewed inter-party talks, distanced itself from any proposals with Hume–Adams fingerprints. The taoiseach on the other hand was determined to salvage the initiative, and if all else failed was prepared to proceed with it on a pan-nationalist as opposed to an intergovernmental basis.

In late November 1993 news broke of the secret British–republican movement dialogue, with much detailed documentation being published on both sides. Coincidentally or otherwise, the British at this point at last came to grips with the Irish proposal and, following a stormy (but decisive) Dublin Castle summit on 3 December, agreed to intensive negotiation to finalise a declaration, about which they remained sceptical but that they felt might not do any harm. In the negotiations, the British were particularly anxious to avoid any ambiguous language that could be misconstrued as an engagement on their part to withdraw from Northern Ireland within any specified time-frame. Two weeks later, on 15 December 1993, prime minister and taoiseach issued the Downing Street Declaration, which transformed the atmosphere.

The declaration bore a discernible resemblance in terms of content to the earlier drafts, but was rounded out and balanced. One crucial advance for which the British were responsible was their offer in the event of a permanent renunciation of violence to treat parties hitherto linked to paramilitaries the same as other political parties in terms of their right to join negotiations on the way ahead. This went beyond the Irish government proposal to establish an inter-party forum, modelled on the New Ireland Forum, which would mark the entry of Sinn Féin into democratic political life.

The Downing Street Declaration was a catalyst for peace. Sinn Féin temporised in response, seeking clarifications, readily given by the Irish government and eventually by the British, before formally rejecting it at the party's Ard Fheis in Letterkenny at the end of July. The clarifications did not involve any renegotiation of the text. While the DUP was opposed, the UUP and the loyalists were not. The Irish back-channel reopened. A number of confidence-building measures were adopted, notably the lifting of the Section 31 broadcasting ban preventing Sinn Féin or IRA spokespersons from giving interviews let alone appearing on the airwaves, and support for a short-term US visa for the president of Sinn Féin to go to America to explain and promote the peace process to its Irish-American supporters. Reynolds dismissed out of hand any notion that he was prepared to settle for anything less than a permanent ceasefire that would subject any negotiation to duress.

On 31 August 1994 a definitive IRA cessation was announced, but, as subsequent events demonstrated, with an unstated mental reservation. A week later, Albert Reynolds, John Hume and Gerry Adams clasped hands on the steps of Government Buildings. The

British government reaction was wary. Within little more than a month, the loyalist paramilitary organisations also declared cease-fires, brokered mainly by Archbishop Eames working with Rev. Roy Magee, but also preceded by a secret meeting between Albert Reynolds and loyalist leaders in Dublin. There was an initial rapid succession of confidence-building gestures, reopening of border roads, selective prisoner releases in the republic, and opening of the Forum for Peace and Reconciliation in Dublin Castle, embracing all parties on the island (including Sinn Féin and Alliance) except the unionist and loyalist ones. President Clinton announced a 1995 Washington economic conference. The two governments prepared to finalise the joint framework document containing the outline of a settlement, as the basis for resumed and enlarged all-party talks.

The decommissioning of weapons also began to raise its head, and in 1995 became a roadblock for talks, exploited by the Ulster Unionist Party, which also rejected the framework document. With the fall of the Reynolds government in November 1994 for uncon-nected reasons, Sinn Féin had to adjust to new Irish government interlocutors. The momentum needed to sustain the peace process slowed down, and eventually the IRA ceasefire itself broke down in February 1996, albeit with only a limited resumption of the IRA campaign and fortunately no loyalist retaliation. It was not nearly as difficult or lengthy a process to reinstate the IRA ceasefire in July 1997, as a prelude to Sinn Féin inclusion in talks, after further changes in government in Britain and Ireland.

The Irish peace process consisted of three phases: the tortu-ous path of establishing ceasefires from the late 1980s to 1994; negotiating a comprehensive political settlement to underpin the ceasefires, which lasted from 1994 to 1998; and, finally, the imple-mentation of the Good Friday Agreement, which took till at least 2010 with progress and interruptions along the way. Courageous political leadership was certainly needed, but also very close coop-eration between civil servants and advisers from different offices and forensic attention to detail. Garret FitzGerald, previously a strong critic of back-channel negotiations, admitted privately that the timing had been right.

Antecedents and Precursors of the Good Friday Agreement

SEAN O ʜUIGINN

Over a decade of my diplomatic career was spent as consul-general in New York and ambassador in Washington, both posts in which much activity related to Northern Ireland policy, but in the marketing rather than in the production department, so to speak. My more direct involvement with policy formation fell into three phases. I spent some years in the late 1970s reporting on unionist opinion through contacts with political, civic and religious leaders from that community. In 1987 I succeeded the redoubtable Michael Lillis as Irish joint secretary in Belfast, heading the very dedicated Irish team he had brought together in the 'Bunker' in Maryfield. Between 1992 and 1997 I was in charge of the Anglo-Irish division of the Department of Foreign Affairs, with responsibilities ranging over the whole spectrum of Anglo-Irish relations, and their American and international out-workings.

The decade from 1987 to 1997 started in great despondency, with justifiable worries that the ever more ruthless spiral of violence could drive society in Northern Ireland into meltdown. However, it proved also an eventful and eventually very fruitful period that supplies a good perspective from which to assess the Good Friday Agreement.

For me, the twentieth anniversary of the agreement celebrates first and foremost a vindication of the much-maligned art of politics. Whatever the judgement of history on the careers of Tony Blair and Bertie Ahern, the consensus must surely be that as regards this particular chapter their contributions could hardly have been bettered for commitment and exemplary cooperation in bringing the agreement over the line. The same applies to the crucial role of Senator George Mitchell, whose extraordinarily patient and judicious chairmanship overcame formidable obstacles to steer the process to success. The Northern political leaders who signed the agreement rose collectively to the highest aspirations of their calling. In Senator George Mitchell's cautious verdict, which remains valid, the agreement did not guarantee peace and stability, but it created the opportunity to accomplish these goals. In other words, the Good Friday Agreement should be viewed not only in terms of what has been achieved, but also for its future potential.

The achievements have been truly impressive. Many lives have undoubtedly been spared. The climate of despair that hung over Northern Ireland has been lifted, and its people can for the most part enjoy the blessing of simple normality in their daily lives. An acceptable police force, which once seemed an impossible dream, is now taken for granted. If there is a fault to be found with the commemoration of the twentieth anniversary, it is that it is not as extensive as it deserves to be, especially perhaps as regards Brexit-torn Britain.

In celebrating the golden moment of the signature of the agreement we must also, however, set it in context. It was not an isolated event, but rather the codification of elements that had been accumulating over decades and reflected the work of many hands. Historians may debate the precise genealogy of accommodation, but the passage of time will only make more evident the continuities involved.

Over the next few years we will be marking the centenaries of a cluster of events that have determined the politics of the island over the past 100 years, including partition. Collectively these events produced a workable degree of stability, but the equilibrium was more in the nature of a stand-off than of a settlement. The patterns of pragmatic agreement or tacit acquiescence they produced were offset and sometimes threatened by deep theoretical chasms on issues of legitimacy, and hedged with patterns of reciprocal denial all round.

These patterns were most acute in relation to Northern Ireland, whose purposeful design to guarantee unionist control succeeded only too well. The permanent monopoly of power on the unionist side and correspondingly permanent disempowerment of the nationalists was a slow-burning fuse, but the explosion meant that the time-honoured patterns of denial had to be revisited on all sides. The past five decades of Anglo-Irish relations can be summarised as a journey, by fits and starts, from stand-off towards settlement. The Good Friday Agreement represents the furthest point to date on that journey.

The journey had three significant milestones, as follows.

- The first was the Sunningdale Agreement, reflecting a belated British recognition that nationalists would no longer accept the role of disempowered and isolated minority assigned to them under the Stormont system. From then onwards, power-sharing and an Irish dimension were seen as indispensable ingredients in the search for accommodation, except obviously by unionist representatives.
- The second was the Anglo-Irish Agreement of 1985. This marked the formal abandonment of the British posture that Dublin's role in relation to Northern Ireland was merely that of any other third country. It acknowledged a formal role for Dublin, through new structures enabling the Irish government to convey views and proposals relating to Northern Ireland. Its other dramatic impact was to make clear that the unionist veto on the sovereignty issue did not extend to all political change, still less to the old assumption that ownership of the flag meant winner took all. Majority rule, even in its passive version of blocking change, was qualified by reference to wider British interests. The tactics of immobilism, shared in spite of their contrasting styles by Ian Paisley and James Molyneaux, no longer amounted to a reliable strategy.
- The third milestone was of course the Good Friday Agreement. It makes sense to deal with the agreement and its immediate

precursors as a unified process, not least because they all flowed from the major policy-shift of the early 1990s, when the governments replaced the goal of isolating republicans with one of including them in political negotiations, subject to their renunciation of violence and espousal of democratic norms.

The republican claim to legitimacy derived from a rump of the second Dáil, who rejected the validity of all subsequent elections and eventually bequeathed its assumed custodianship of Irish sovereignty, as a farmer might a smallholding, to the IRA army council. The IRA chief of staff thereby became a kind of hidden imam of legitimate Irish rule. This reasoning would have been comic except that people were willing to kill and be killed in its name. The combination of magical thinking and ruthless violence isolated republicans from all strands of constitutional or even rational politics on the island, and such power as the IRA garnered from its myth remained purely negative and sterile.

The incentives to devolution built in to the Anglo-Irish Agreement foundered initially on unionist rage, but gradually unionists came to the sober realisation that more was required to defend their interests than variations on the theme of 'no'. These tendencies were deftly fostered by Secretary of State Brooke, leading to the Brooke–Mayhew talks (1991–2), the most ambitious since Sunningdale.

Republicans have always rejected any suggestion that their actions were influenced by the Anglo-Irish Agreement. However, in the dialogue between the SDLP and Sinn Féin in the late 1980s it furnished the central plank of John Hume's argument that the 'armed struggle'—leaving aside any issues of morality—was misguided and counterproductive on purely pragmatic grounds. If the British presence in Ireland was now motivated only by a concern not to repudiate the unionist allegiance of a majority in Northern Ireland, it followed that the key to Irish unity lay in persuading that majority; not in violence aimed at an outdated notion of British imperialism.

The outcome of the dialogue seemed merely to crystallise the familiar differences between the two parties. What was new and significant, however, was that the republican presentation had abandoned the tone of haughty *fatwa*, and offered political arguments that accepted implicitly that its policies needed rational justification. The radical shift in Irish government policy of the early 1990s was not so much a change of heart on their part as a response to a republican change of tone, giving some hope, diligently fostered by John Hume, that republicans might abandon the campaign of violence and make the unambiguous democratic commitment that would enable them to be included in negotiations.

The relative success of the peace process has led people to forget how controversial that change in government policy was. Its consolidation by the Fianna Fáil/Labour coalition (1993–4), with Taoiseach Albert Reynolds supported in all essential respects by Tánaiste Dick Spring, evinced a high degree of political courage on their part. There was a body of opinion in the state that assumed optimistically that a policy of resolute non-involvement with Northern Ireland would ensure that its problems stayed comfortably at bay. The back issues of the *Sunday Independent*, which marshalled its writers in a strident weekly chorus excoriating Hume and his dupes, illustrate the depth of opposition the new policy departure could evoke. The government was in fact fully aware of the risks, but felt they were justified on several grounds, rightly as I believed.

Hume's entire career was governed by his visceral opposition to political violence and had established his reputation as a formidable political strategist. I felt the government owed it to his record to explore constructively his insistent view that the opportunity now existed for a new drive for peace.

The policy of uniting the moderates across the divide so as to isolate their respective extremes was sensible in every respect, with one exception. It had not worked in any of the forms that had been tried. The moderates feared their own extremes more than they trusted their presumed fellow moderates. Invited to swing their political trapeze across the tribal divide, they had no confidence that they would be grasped by supporting arms in mid-air, and justifiable fears that their ropes might be slashed from behind. Since peace had not been found through politics, it was time to try whether politics could be found through peace.

Moreover, the unremitting violence was growing ever more intolerable and it was becoming ever more urgent to stop it. That could be attempted by recourse to a new panoply of exceptional security measures to repress the paramilitaries by military means, or, alternatively, through negotiations aimed at persuading them to desist voluntarily.

Both carried risks for the government's democratic credentials and the rule of law. Irish history is replete with instances in which military repression proved counterproductive, and there was no guarantee that drastic new emergency measures would escape this pattern. There was the opposite risk that negotiations with the paramilitaries could be seen as a capitulation to terrorism, compromising democratic values in another way. I felt this latter risk was manageable through careful attention to the preconditions for negotiations. I did not share the fear that the apparent change in republican attitudes was just a cynical tactical feint. Organisations rarely put core values into play for tactical gambits.

The search for progress on Northern Ireland was now proceeding on two levels: one public, and one initially out of public sight.

The Brooke–Mayhew talks were beset by procedural wrangling and deep divisions on the substantive issues. Nevertheless they were very valuable in setting procedural templates and discarding taboos in ways that greatly facilitated the subsequent negotiations under Senator Mitchell.

They failed, however, to bridge any substantive gaps. On strand 1 the SDLP made a very high bid for a six-person Northern Ireland executive, three of whom would be directly elected, the others appointed by the British and Irish governments and the European Union (EU) respectively. The unionists offered neither power-sharing nor a formal Irish dimension. They proposed the oversight of Stormont departments by chairpersons of assembly committees, selected according to electoral strength, one of whom would be empowered to deal with the Irish government on an ad-hoc basis.

On strand 2 the unionists demanded an unconditional pledge from the Irish government to remove the territorial claim to Northern Ireland from the Irish constitution. The Irish government questioned this one-dimensional view of the constitution and said that as a practical matter, winning the necessary referendum would need a context of more assured respect for the rights and identity of northern nationalists. This stance met with much criticism, and not just from unionists. Irish ministers were conscious that in the nature of things, any future package would contain mostly elements of compromise that unionists would find wanting when judged against the gold standard of the old Stormont. Changing the Irish constitution was a rare prospect of unalloyed gain for them, and it made no sense to devalue it in the foothills of negotiation.

When the Brooke–Mayhew talks fizzled out and the John Hume–Gerry Adams negotiations became public, some argued that the Irish government and Hume had regarded the Brooke–Mayhew talks as mere theatre, and had neglected opportunities for progress in favour of the more comprehensive process they were pursuing. This was never the case, since the government saw the two exercises as entirely complementary, and regarded any elements of agreement that could be achieved in the talks as valuable assets for a future process involving the republicans, if indeed one could be achieved.

The Brooke–Mayhew talks had Sunningdale as a template. The negotiations that flowed from the Hume–Adams dialogue, by contrast, were in uncharted territory and much more challenging both in principle and in practice. To enter negotiations, the republicans had to meet certain essential preconditions, notably a complete and unambiguous renunciation of violence. On the other hand, if the republican leaders were to persuade their followers to cross the proffered bridge into purely democratic negotiations, the terms had to be compatible with their political aspirations but without driving others from the table.

Contrary to public impressions at the time, the dialogue between Hume and Adams did not produce tablets of stone that were then handed to the Irish government. It provided rather the impetus for a floating drafting process, drawing on the work of the two men but then amended by many hands. Since the objective was a joint statement that would enable an IRA ceasefire, the terms had to be acceptable to both governments. It was refined by a very small group of officials from both sides, of which I was one, led by the two Cabinet secretaries, Sir Robin Butler and the late Dermot Nally.

The core element was Hume's creative treatment of self-determination, which affirmed that right for the Irish people as a whole, but qualified it by acknowledging that disagreement between them as to its application had to be overcome by peaceful persuasion if Irish unity was to be achieved. This cast the reality in terms more compatible with republican doctrines, by treating the consent principle as a subset of the principle of self-determination rather than as a denial of it. This was buttressed by British acceptance of these principles, and the pledge to legislate impartially for whatever option was freely chosen by the greater number in Northern Ireland. It defined the British role as one of promoting agreement based on mutual respect. The Irish government made corresponding undertakings on reconciliation and mutual respect, with particular emphasis on allaying unionist concerns, and pledged as part of a balanced accommodation to support change in the Irish constitution to fully respect the principle of consent. Both governments affirmed the need for a permanent end to paramilitary violence but confirmed significantly that all democratically mandated parties that established a commitment to purely peaceful methods would be free to participate fully in negotiations.

True to their immemorial reputation as tricky negotiators, the British, in preparation for the Anglo-Irish summit planned for early December 1993, advanced a boiler-plate alternative text that would have amounted to a provocative rebuff to the entire peace effort. Fortunately, after an extraordinarily fraught summit, Prime Minister John Major agreed to continue working on the basis elaborated over the previous year, leading to the Downing Street Declaration later that month.

The declaration brought the two governments closer than ever before to bridging the theoretical gaps dividing them. Its rhetoric was a strong plea for a liberating spirit of mutual respect to replace past suspicions. Albert Reynolds's quiet outreach to unionists through respected clergymen had helped to moderate the UUP and loyalist response. Even Dr Paisley delivered only low-calibre anathemas. Republicans pronounced the declaration inadequate, and demanded clarifications. Eight frustrating months elapsed before it finally achieved its tacit objective of an IRA ceasefire.

In the wake of the ceasefire it was the turn of the British government to play for time, through semantic debate on permanence and other contrivances. It was clear that John Major now found the promise of negotiations within three months of a complete ceasefire, which he had held out to the republicans, either uncomfortable or impossible to deliver.

In early 1995 British delaying tactics took an altogether more unsettling form, when they advanced prior decommissioning as a precondition for Sinn Féin participation in negotiations. The Irish government had always seen decommissioning as an essential strategic goal of the process, but presented in practical rather than symbolic terms as a corollary of political agreement. To demand it up front for delaying purposes, as a symbolic test that the republicans could not pass, was deeply counterproductive for the goal itself and corrosive of trust in British intentions. Whatever forces had sought to dissuade Major from the Downing Street Declaration had not gone away, and had found a sure way of breaking the momentum of the peace process.

As often happens, the tactic took on a life of its own and much energy, which would have been better expended in consolidating progress, went instead towards overcoming this obstacle to political negotiations. The inordinate delay in launching them clearly ran counter to the understanding that had led to the ceasefire and was causing obvious strains in republican ranks. I recall we were in a plane over the Atlantic after a trip to Washington where Dick Spring felt he had significantly advanced the prospects for talks when we got word of the Canary Wharf bombing (9 February 1996). It was a very bitter setback, requiring all calculations to be reset.

In November 1995 the governments had decided to refer the decommissioning crux to an international commission, eventually chaired by Senator Mitchell. Its report, published shortly before Canary Wharf, set the issue in a more practical context, proposing six principles to test democratic commitment instead of the simplistic yardstick of decommissioning, and suggesting a more gradual schedule for the latter. It also gave qualified endorsement to the idea of an election to decide participants in talks, which the SDLP had opposed because of the delay and potential polarisation it could involve, but the UUP saw as a route to sidestep the decommissioning block. In accepting the Mitchell report, Major placed his main emphasis on the general election that ensued in May 1997. Talks began without Sinn Féin shortly afterwards.

The interval since the IRA ceasefire had seen action by the governments to provide a 'peace dividend' to both the paramilitaries and the general population, through prisoner releases and easing of irksome measures occasioned by the security threat. In a framework document published in 1995, to give impetus to the political debate, they had also developed a model for the possible outworking of the Downing Street Declaration, through new institutions broadly on Sunningdale lines but with greater emphasis on parity of esteem and a clearer foreshadowing of the change in the Irish constitution that was eventually implemented. The framework envisaged participation in north–south institutions as a duty of service for northern ministers, and, in the event of collapse of the process, the governments would seek other ways to carry forward the necessary cooperation, implying a limit to unionist capacity to block change.

Unionist reaction to the threat of unwelcome change had taken the form of brandishing more insistently the now hollow symbols of their old supremacy, notably in an intense annual confrontation surrounding Orange marches to Drumcree Church, which had assumed a symbolic importance out of all proportion to the issue at stake. Meanwhile the campaign of violence continued to sacrifice the lives or well-being of innocent victims to make a political point.

Towards the end of John Major's premiership it was evident that his capacity for initiative on Northern Ireland had shrunk to the point where any action he might take would be so deep inside the unionist comfort zone as to be useless for reaching wider agreement. Irish diplomacy was essentially defensive at that stage, aimed at preventing earlier gains from unravelling rather than hoping for new advances.

The British and Irish electoral cycles, which had often stymied progress, were for once in benign alignment when elections in both countries in 1997 brought to power two new governments with fresh mandates and heightened commitment to restore momentum to the search for agreement.

In autumn of 1997 I took up appointment as ambassador to Washington.

Looking back on my decade of direct involvement in the peace process, I take pride in having served governments who sought with commendable courage and vision to pursue a potentially risky new path to peace, initially in the teeth of the conventional political wisdom. They did so rigorously and thoughtfully, creating a bridge into peaceful politics for violent republicanism without ever compromising their own democratic credentials. Albert Reynolds and Dick Spring used their strategic talents to map the railway line leading to agreement. If the train was not moving due to the constraints on John Major towards the end of his term, neither had it been let roll down the embankment. It stood ready for Bertie Ahern's peerless tactical skills to drive it to its destination, in harmony with a British prime minister, Tony Blair, who was fortunately both committed and empowered.

The Good Friday Agreement has been criticised for its failings on several grounds, but in most cases these arise less from unforeseen consequences than from choices that, for better or worse, were thought necessary to meet the particular circumstances of Northern Ireland.

The charge that the agreement entrenches rather than transcends sectarian divisions reflects a dilemma that had arisen earlier on fair employment legislation. It was felt then that where sectarian classification is a key informal principle of social organisation, legislation to prevent the ensuing abuses will only get a real purchase if it takes explicit legal cognisance of this pervasive social reality. The same reasoning applied to the wider political reality dealt with in the Good Friday Agreement. Moreover, most aspects of the agreement could in practice be changed by cross-community consensus, so we felt the problems of the cure would not outlast the disease.

The cumbersome procedures to cater for power-sharing are another case in point. The 'on–off' record of devolved government is perhaps the single greatest source of despondency about the agreement. Both the DUP and Sinn Féin leadership tend to treat operation of the Northern Ireland Assembly as just another object for gestural politics rather than a necessary framework. Northern Ireland Secretary Peter Mandelson's decision to use suspension of the assembly as the 'naughty step' regarding decommissioning (strongly against the advice of Dublin) set an unfortunate precedent in this regard. Compared to the Himalayas that have been climbed in the process so far, the present obstacles are in the Sperrins range (mountains in County Tyrone) and could easily be overcome by resolute joint governmental action, once London finally escapes the paralysis of Brexit.

The deepest value of the agreement is not the enabling of devolution or even the institutional reforms it has successfully achieved. It is rather that it has set out agreed ground rules to govern the process of change that are buttressed by treaty and endorsed by referendums encompassing the whole population of the island. This makes the situation post-agreement qualitatively different and vastly better than what obtained before.

This dimension is all the more important as the process of change in Northern Ireland is gathering pace. The sense throughout the western world is of old certainties eroding without new ones yet in place. Predictions everywhere have become conjectural as never before. Even the integrity of the quarrel of Churchill's famous dreary steeples may no longer prove immune to the general volatility.

The negative role of Brexit will depend on how much it convulses the pattern of relationships that flowed from British EU membership and were assumed as a given in the agreement, which would otherwise have been replete with contingency provisions. The Brexit soup will probably not be served as hot as it is being cooked, given the intractable realities involved. Even if it is, the assumption that unionists who oppose Brexit are thereby ready to espouse Irish unity is fatuous. The constitutional issue in Northern Ireland will inexorably become a game of margins, however, and even a small sliver of the population swayed by Brexit could prove significant.

The likeliest threat to stability in Northern Ireland may be less from some sudden lurch to a united Ireland than from unionists' reaction when they fully realise that just as Irish unity could come about only by those who favoured it persuading those who do not, the maintenance of the union will increasingly depend on the same principle. That could be traumatic for a community hard-wired to believe that its freedom is synonymous with its control, and will call for wise leadership to forestall a reflex of disengagement and disaffection from Northern Ireland on that community's part.

Ironically, unionists may find that their surest guarantee against being railroaded lies in the hated Irish dimension. A referendum in the north in favour of unity will need a referendum in the south for its implementation. Unionist attitudes will be very important in the latter regard, both for voters determined not to repeat the mistakes of the old Stormont in dismissing the needs of a minority and for those, less nobly perhaps, who simply want to keep northern disruption at bay. There could well be a protracted period of uncertainty and a need for a kind of decompression chamber to allow for an orderly adaptation to change.

It is commonplace to speak of the ambiguity of the Good Friday Agreement and related documents. In fact this is a misnomer. Their language, although occasionally convoluted, rarely if ever admits of contradictory meanings simultaneously. What is really meant is that the provisions can apply indifferently to the contradictory alternatives of the union or Irish unity. Measures to respect the divided allegiances of Northern Ireland are already pledged to continue with reversed polarity in the event of a change of flag. This dimension of the agreement is rarely discussed, but historians of the future may well regard this and the principles underpinning it as one of the agreement's most significant contributions to the orderly management of change.

Weak Tea and Shortbread: Reflections on the Northern Ireland Peace Process

FERGUS FINLAY

I was sort of plonked into the peace process in early 1992, and it immediately presented me with a crisis of conscience.

After the formation of the Reynolds/Spring government, and somewhat to the surprise of the people around him, Dick Spring opted to become minister for Foreign Affairs, and I went with him as his political adviser. He made that choice because he knew, from conversations with Taoiseach Albert Reynolds, that there was a 'peace project' under way.

It took me a little while to settle into Iveagh House—they have ways of making political advisers feel welcome, and one of them was to offer me an office that was as far removed from the tánaiste's as it was possible to be. Once those initial difficulties were overcome, and they began, hesitantly, to take me into their confidence, I was given some of the files to read.

That was the shocking part. It quickly became clear that there had been an ongoing dialogue involving Sinn Féin and the Provisional IRA—the Provos. I remember having to find out what the references to BAC were in some of the letters the IRA had sent—not realising that in their terms, BAC—Baile Átha Cliath, the Irish for Dublin—meant the Irish government.

I had worked in politics for more than ten years at that point—throughout the period of the New Ireland Forum and the negotiation of the Anglo-Irish Agreement of 1985. The politics that I knew—and to which I was committed—had at its heart the aim of enabling nationalism to gather itself around a sense of purpose that excluded the Provos, and that was aimed at trying to strengthen the political centre, with the aim of ensuring that the Provos and the 'armed struggle' could wither on the vine.

If you subscribe to that sort of political activity and purpose, and then overnight discover that a totally different, and completely subterranean, approach had been followed since the late 1980s, it's not easy to get your head around it. The aim of this different approach was to do precisely the opposite—to bring the Provos in from the margins to the centre of the discussion, in the hope that the people who had been seen as the problem could be made part of the solution.

And this was happening while violence continued unabated. When he had been foreign minister for 80 days, Dick Spring addressed a Labour Party conference in Waterford. He started his leader's address to that conference by reading out a long list of names of people who had been killed since he became minister. Twenty-seven people in 80 days, ranging in age from 19 to 58.

It took several minutes to read in front of a packed, sombre and quiet hall. It included the name of Julie Statham, which I will never forget. She took her own life after her boyfriend was killed in an IRA attack. It also included the names of Johnathan Ball and Tim Parry, three- and twelve-year-old boys who had been killed by shrapnel in Warrington when the Provos placed bombs in litter-bins made of metal.

So the work that became my understanding of the Anglo-Irish process was book-ended at the start by the Warrington bomb and punctuated along the way by atrocity upon atrocity.

And yet there was an inescapable logic to it. The previous process—the one that I and many others believed in—had failed. Violence hadn't stopped; the Provos hadn't withered away. It was necessary to do what John Hume, Martin Mansergh and others did—to engage directly with the source of the violence. And it did result in the letter from the Provos—the BAC letter, I always call it —that led to the negotiating process of the Downing Street Declaration.

That process in turn meant that more or less every second week, we went to the Northern Ireland Office in London, and every other week they came to Iveagh House. Each meeting concerned itself with tiny bits of text —what we came to call terms of art. A term of art is something that you've now agreed. You set it in stone. It cannot be changed, and you might take weeks and weeks to negotiate it.

The process—which ultimately led to the Downing Street Declaration after more than a year of meetings—involved ideas and language that had no status until they were agreed between both sides. Sometimes we were negotiating around something called an angel paper—a British term. It's an idea the British side puts forward—if you don't like it, it dematerialises. It disappears. It never had any status.

When it's agreed, it becomes a term of art. Phrases like 'no selfish strategic or economic interest', 'their right of self-determination on the basis of consent', and many others were discussed again and again—sometimes with a lot of abstruse discussion about the meaning or place of a comma.

One phrase proved impossible to reconcile. In the negotiations that followed the Downing Street Declaration, and that led to the joint framework documents, there was significant disagreement about the difference between 'parity of esteem and equality of treatment' (the Irish preference) and 'parity of esteem and equity of treatment' (the British version). At one meeting, one of the British officials explained that in equality of treatment, everyone gets what they want, whereas in equity of treatment everyone gets what they deserve. We never resolved that disagreement, and the key phrase that appeared in the documents in the end was 'parity of esteem and treatment'—probably a neat enough compromise!

It has to be said that there were many times in the course of that process when it felt like a complete fool's errand. The darkest time was in October 1993—the week following the Shankill massacre. The IRA exploded a bomb in a fish shop called Frizzell's—apparently believing that a UDA meeting was taking place upstairs. The bomb detonated prematurely and killed nine people, including one of the IRA members who had carried it in.

That massacre, on a Saturday when secret negotiations about the Downing Street Declaration were at their most intense, was followed by fourteen murders of Catholics in reprisal, including eight shot dead in a pub in Greysteel, Co. Derry. Apart from the reprisals, there was a palpable sense of shock when Gerry Adams carried the coffin of the bomber who had died on the Shankill, Thomas Begley.

That sequence of events almost derailed the entire process. Angry and bitter debates took place in the House of Commons— in the course of one of them John Major said:

> If the implication of his remarks is that we should sit down and talk with Mr. Adams and the Provisional IRA, I can say only that that would turn my stomach and those of most honourable Members; we will not do it. If and when there is a total ending of violence, and if and when that ending of violence is established for a significant time, we shall talk to all the constitutional parties that have people elected in their names. I will not talk to people who murder indiscriminately.

In the debate that took place in the Dáil after the massacre, Dick Spring made a speech that was regarded as having put the process back on track. He outlined six principles that had to be the measure of progress.

1. The people living in Ireland, north and south, without coercion and without violence, should be free to determine their own future.
2. Freedom can be expressed in the development of new structures—internal to Northern Ireland, north/south, and east/west.
3. No agreement can be reached in respect of any change in the present status of Northern Ireland

without the freely expressed consent of a majority of the people of Northern Ireland.

4. Acceptance that the freedom of unionists to consent to constitutional change also means the freedom of unionists to withhold their consent from such change, unless and until they are persuaded by democratic political means only.

5. If we believe in consent as an integral part of any democratic approach to peace, we must be prepared at the right time and in the right circumstances to express our commitment to that consent in our fundamental law.

6. Even in the aftermath of some of the most horrible crimes we have witnessed, we must be prepared to say to the men of violence that they can come to the negotiating table, that they can play a peaceful part in the development of Ireland's future, if only they will stop the killing, and maiming and the hurting.

He ended that speech—and the debate—by saying:

> There is a heavy onus now on all democrats. Now is one of those moments in our history when we choose to go forward or backward. As someone who was elected to speak on behalf of a new generation, I say 'we must go forward'.

After that immensely difficult moment the process got under way again, and was to culminate in the Downing Street Declaration and ultimately the first IRA ceasefire. The six principles ultimately found their way into the joint framework documents, and remain a succinct underpinning of a lot of progress since.

In terms of my own role in that period, I often reflect that while Sean O hUiginn seldom had an 'off-the-record' encounter that didn't involve a cardinal, and Martin Mansergh's interlocutors included internationally renowned terrorists, I spent many nights travelling to vicars' houses in different parts of Northern Ireland, speaking to really, really polite groups of unionists.

I did that so often and I did it to such numbing effect that I became convinced that there is somewhere in the heart of Northern Ireland a Protestant factory that makes very, very dry shortbread and very, very weak tea. For the best part of a year that was my diet at least twice a week.

I did have a number of perhaps more consequential meetings —including one with members of the Combined Loyalist Military Command at which they gave me a set of human-rights declarations that ultimately found their way into the Downing Street Declaration.

There were two things I particularly remember about that first meeting. I can still recall my anxiety when I was told I was to meet Gusty Spence, because my only image of Spence was of this lantern-jawed figure wearing a woolly hat and cradling a Kalashnikov. I was completely unprepared for the avuncular, twinkly-eyed figure I actually met. As I got to know him slightly I came to the conclusion that of all the people I met in that period, Gusty Spence was the one who had made the most complete change in his heart away from violence, and he had led a significant group of people away from violence because he had learnt the futility of it for himself.

David Ervine was with him that day, and he was another who made a huge impression on me. One thing he said never left me. 'I can't understand,' he said, 'why people like you want me to feel less British, in order that you can feel more Irish.'

A somewhat less avuncular figure I met in that period was Billy Wright, who gloried in the nickname 'King Rat'. I've written in more detail about that encounter elsewhere, but I can still remember the feeling that I might be lucky to survive the day. At the end of our meeting he told me that when everyone else got five minutes' warning, I'd get fifteen—his way of saying (I think) that we were friends now.

There were many other processes before my involvement was done. The negotiations of the joint framework documents, was, if anything, more difficult. From the Irish end those negotiations were carried in the main by Dick Spring, and I honestly believe they were his greatest achievement.

There is a direct line of descent and progress from the Downing Street Declaration—the statement of principles—to the joint framework documents, which put essential flesh on the bones of the declaration. The Good Friday Agreement would not have been possible without the agenda and solutions posited by the joint framework documents. And those documents were negotiated with a British government, led by John Major, that had a parlous existence, because it had no majority in the Commons. The political vicissitudes of the period—which included a change of government here in Ireland—required an extraordinary degree of tenacity and skill on the part of Dick Spring.

He went from being regarded as the 'soft on unionism' side of the Fianna Fáil/Labour government (1993–94) to being seen as the green edge of the Fine Gael/Labour government (1994–97). In reality, his position never changed. He often described the aim of the process during that period as being 'to get the violence out of the conflict'. Indeed, a variant of that phrase can be found in the joint framework documents, where it says 'A climate of peace enables the process of healing to begin.'

A fuller and more complete account of my own involvement would have to include other adventures. But it's not possible to leave the subject without saying something about Albert Reynolds.

There are certain quarters in which I am regarded as having played a significant—and indeed a somewhat villainous—role in Albert Reynolds's downfall. That's another story, not really capable of being dealt with here. But when it came to the Anglo-Irish end of the peace process—the bit I know best—Reynolds's contribution was unique and beyond measure.

I had worked in Garret FitzGerald's government in the 1980s. I was familiar with the way in which Haughey's government went about things. These governments got involved in process in different ways, and process ended up mattering. Sometimes for its own sake. The process was what you did on a day-to-day basis, and you tried to do it to the best of your ability. And as long as you were doing that, you didn't have to devote too much thought to outcomes.

Albert Reynolds had no interest in process. It very quickly became clear (to me at any rate) that he had a simple, singular, objective. To stop the violence.

A couple of days before the IRA ceasefire actually happened, after months of wearying negotiations about text, Reynolds met an influential delegation from America who were heading north to deliver final messages to the IRA leadership. In their meeting with Albert there was talk about guns and weapons and so on, and one of the Americans said, 'Well of course they certainly have to keep defensive weapons.' Albert looked him straight in the eye and said, 'No weapons, no weapons. People at peace don't need weapons. They don't need defensive weapons. They don't need any weapons. I want you to tell them in words that a primary school student will understand. This is about putting the guns away.'

I could give other examples of his directness, but suffice it to say that I believe his singular objective was what gave that phase of the process meaning. He had a very clear, very simple, and absolutely monumental outcome in mind.

I don't think we'd have got to a Downing Street declaration and I don't think we'd have got to an IRA ceasefire if it hadn't been for the fact that Albert Reynolds had that one singular objective in mind. If you have a process that becomes process for its own sake it's guaranteed to go on forever. If you have a process that's skilful and patient and honest, but that reports to a political leader who is committed to an outcome, you have a chance of getting somewhere.

Nobody can argue—and I certainly wouldn't—that Albert Reynolds got everything right. He made decisions later that were destructive and corrosive of trust. But I don't believe it's possible to reflect honestly on that period without saying one thing. If you ever want to put up a monument to the people who got the guns out of our age-old conflict, put it up to Albert Reynolds and the team around him at the time.

Panel 3 Overview

CATHERINE DAY

In politics, timing is everything. This panel session illustrated this old adage by showing how opportunities can be created and seized when the time is right, and how the best of ideas can stall when the timing is not auspicious.

The panel brought together former political advisers Martin Mansergh and Fergus Finlay with former civil servant Sean O hUiginn. While it underlined the different roles they had played, it was striking to hear how closely a handful of advisers and civil servants worked together in unconventional ways in search of a sustainable peace process. Although they each felt that the process of building confidence one step at a time had been important, they also spoke about the risks that different politicians had taken in pursuit of peace. They described the highs and lows of the decade of the 1990s, which bridged the time between the Anglo-Irish Agreement of 1985 and the Good Friday Agreement.

KEY PERSONALITIES

They highlighted the role of key individuals, often churchmen, who acted as go-betweens, enabling discussions that could not have taken place in the open because of the difficult security background and many atrocities. Martin Mansergh divided the peace process into three phases: establishing ceasefires from the late 1980s to 1994, negotiating a comprehensive political agreement to underpin the ceasefires from 1994 to 1998, and then the implementation of the Good Friday Agreement until at least 2010. He traced the key features of the Anglo-Irish Agreement of 1985 and the basis that it laid for future progress. He went on to speak of the role played by Fr Alex Reid, a Redemptorist priest who, with the backing of Cardinal Ó Fiaich, had tried to bring nationalists together in the search for peace. Mansergh explained that Charlie Haughey had first met Fr Reid while still in opposition in 1986. He said Haughey had contemplated meeting John Hume and Gerry Adams in the autumn of 1987 but that the security situation culminating in the Enniskillen bombing made that impossible.

Following the entry of the SDLP into a public dialogue with Sinn Féin in 1988, at the request of Fr Reid and on the instruction of Charlie Haughey (who had since become taoiseach in February 1987), Mansergh attended a meeting in the Redemptorist monastery in Dundalk. Over the next eighteen months he participated in meetings at six-week intervals with Martin McGuinness. The meetings worked on a joint declaration of principles.

THE PROCESS

Mansergh spoke about the process of developing exchanges and draft documents and the need for direct dialogue and confidence-building. This sometimes led to direct meetings with Martin McGuinness and his associate(s). He said he was conscious of the taboo on 'talking to terrorists' but felt that it had to be overcome to make progress. He also spoke of his feeling of responsibility to the democratic system and of the obligations accepted under the Anglo-Irish Agreement.

By 1991 the multiple contacts had led to the preparation of a draft statement by the taoiseach and British prime minister. By then Haughey was in his last months as taoiseach. He raised the prospect of a draft statement in a meeting with Prime Minister John Major in Dublin in December 1991, but was unable to take it forward. Haughey was succeeded by Albert Reynolds. Fergus Finlay described being taken aback on starting work with Tánaiste Dick Spring in

1992 to discover that, instead of trying to strengthen the centre ground of nationalism and to exclude the Provos, contacts had been taking place aimed at including the Provos as part of the solution. He described Albert Reynolds as 'the first taoiseach ... who had one objective in mind', namely ending the violence. Finlay went on to say that he did not think the Downing Street Declaration could have been achieved without that clear focus of Reynolds on the objective of ending violence that had helped bring about the IRA ceasefire.

Sean O hUiginn described his role as a 'traveller' in the 1970s and the 'utmost courtesy' shown to him in all his dealings with the unionist side at that time. Subsequently in the late 1980s he was appointed joint secretary 'in the bunker' (the Anglo-Irish secretariat in Maryfield). He spoke about two factors in the peace process: first, the direct line of continuity in the entire Anglo-Irish Northern Ireland process, which he described as a 'genealogy of accommodation which is refined, taken from one generation to the next'; and second, the fact that progress took a long time because at every stage one or the other participant was in denial.

He spoke about the process as a journey from stand-off to settlement, with the Good Friday Agreement being the 'closest to settlement that we've ever had'. He argued that 'taking out denial' was a crucial factor in bringing about agreement on power-sharing. He said that the Good Friday Agreement took the British out of the biggest part of their denial, in thinking that 'Dublin was like Bulgaria in terms of its relevance to Northern Ireland', and led to the recognition of an obligation of partnership in managing the problem. Referring to devolution and political dialogue, he recalled that the unionists, having 'tried the tested means of demonstration, street demonstration and so on', found that it did not help them to get a purchase on the intergovernmental discussion and so they began to develop means of dialogue. He also highlighted the fact that, at that time, the republican constituency was outside the ambit of the talks, and spoke about the 'apparently contradictory concepts of self-determination for Ireland and the principle of consent for unionists'.

Sean O hUiginn paid tribute to the role of Peter Brooke as a 'very subtle and deft politician'. Commenting on how the incentives to devolution built into the Anglo-Irish Agreement 'foundered initially on unionist rage', he said unionists gradually came to the sober realisation that more was required to defend their interests than variations on the theme of 'no'. These tendencies were 'deftly fostered' by Mr Brooke, leading to the Brooke/Mayhew talks (1991–92), which he described as 'the most ambitious since Sunningdale'. Although these talks were beset by procedural wrangling, O hUiginn said they were valuable in setting procedural templates and discarding taboos, which later facilitated negotiations under Senator George Mitchell.

O hUiginn also referred to signs of a change of heart in the republican community in the late 1980s, illustrated by the documents published by the SDLP and Sinn Féin. He said the texts were 'very interesting partly because they cover a lot of the agenda that was subsequently to become familiar but also because for the first time you could see a change of tone'. He went on to say that during the period Sinn Féin became involved in rational dialogue for the first time, and that was when John Hume sensed there was a possibility of a sea-change.

Although many commentators argued that such an apparent change was just tactics, O hUiginn said he felt that organisations do not generally put 'absolutely core values into play for tactical purposes' and that he was convinced the change was real. Although he knew the dangers of 'accommodating a terrorist movement and of contaminating democratic politics', he personally felt that the possibility of a voluntary ending of violence was such an enormous prize that the risk was worth taking—a view shared by Albert Reynolds and Dick Spring. He stressed that when embarking on this course of action there was 'no sense of certainty that the outreach to Sinn Féin would be successful'. He was concerned that the talks might fail, not because of bad faith but 'in all good faith'.

O hUiginn discussed the criticism at that time of the Irish government for not putting articles 2 and 3 of the Irish constitution on the table. He took the view that if there was to be a grand bargain with the unionists, there would have to be 'a trophy of some considerable dimensions' and this should not be given away in what he called the foothills of the negotiations.

Returning to the issue of weapons, he explained that the Irish government had to distinguish between what was not negotiable and what was presentational. He took the view that decommissioning was not a question of principle but a tactic by John Major, who was unable to bring his Tory supporters along with him. O hUiginn commented that it was a 'great tragedy that they used a strategic objective for a tactical purpose'. Looking back on the 1990s, he felt that at least a template had been developed for bringing the republicans into the political negotiation. The Downing Street Declaration was important because it narrowed the gap between the two governments, and 'because of good diplomacy by both Albert Reynolds and John Major it was not aggressively contested by any party'.

THE ROLE OF THE AMERICANS

The panel also discussed the role of the USA in the peace process during the 1990s. Sean O hUiginn spoke about the disproportion of power between London and Dublin and the importance of the work done by John Hume, Michael Lillis and Seán Donlon in the US, which effectively gave 'a democratic lever to the Irish government that everybody including the Provos could understand'. He added 'without the American dimension I don't think there would have been a successful peace process'. Fergus Finlay spoke of the role played by Bill Clinton in securing a US visa for Gerry Adams at a critical moment. Tribute was also paid to the roles of George Mitchell and of the US ambassador to Ireland, Jean Kennedy Smith, during these years.

COMMENTS FROM THE FLOOR

Opening the discussion from the floor, Declan O'Donovan commented that the first great success of the Anglo-Irish Agreement was the ending of the supergrass trials. He recalled that, following his appointment to the Anglo-Irish Secretariat in 1989, he was called to a meeting with Taoiseach Charlie Haughey. Haughey took the time to tell him that, despite not being 'exactly in favour of the Anglo-Irish Agreement', he wanted O'Donovan to 'go up there and implement it to the hilt'. Haughey added that 'we want to keep the British to their promises' and underlined the importance of the agreement being seen to work. Reflecting on his time in Maryfield, O'Donovan remarked on the courage of Adams and McGuinness, who, at that time, 'had by no means control over their own people and … were in danger of their lives'. He felt that the role played by Peter Brooke was probably under-reported and that Brooke had been in a unique position to be able to handle 'something that was going to cause fluttering of the Tory party'. He quoted from Brooke's 'Whitbread speech' of November 1990 in which he said that Britain had 'no selfish strategic or economic interest' in Northern Ireland—a line that was repeated in the Downing Street Declaration. Without wanting to take away from the role played by Albert Reynolds, he took the view that the process had started under Haughey and Thatcher.

Chris Hudson, a Unitarian Church minister from Belfast, spoke about his dialogue with the loyalists and the UVF. He highlighted the importance of reassuring the loyalist side that there would not be a secret deal, thus enabling them to keep their communities calm. He also spoke about contacts between Proinsias De Rossa and John Bruton that culminated in Bruton agreeing to include a message to the loyalist community in a speech he made to the joint houses of the US Senate and Congress. He paid tribute to Joe Brosnan, former secretary general of the Department of Justice, and his work with the Independent Monitoring Commission.

Philip McDonagh spoke about the transition in the UK from John Major to Tony Blair. He focused on the question of what self-determination would mean in the context of an eventual agreement and how the Labour Party would handle such issues. He spoke about continuing the outreach to the unionist community, first with James Molyneaux and later with David Trimble, whereby one of the key issues was the stability of a future agreement (the term 'moving staircase' was used at this time). McDonagh also referred to the issue of prisoners, including the case of Róisín McAliskey. The first official contact the Irish embassy in London had with Sinn Féin was through a visit by Gerry Adams in September 1994 at which Adams stressed the importance of the prisoners. This led to McDonagh being encouraged to visit UK prisons, beginning in 1995.

Hugh Logue and Frank Cogan spoke about the role the EU had played in supporting the peace process, both financially and politically. Logue spoke about Bill Clinton's references to regular phone calls with Jacques Chirac, president of France, which always included calls for US support to help Northern Ireland. Cogan spoke about providing copies of the Anglo-Irish Agreement to every member of the European Parliament, only to be denounced by Ian Paisley MEP for interfering. He also spoke about the financial support from the EU that funded flanking measures that supported the peace process. Martin Mansergh referred to the inspiration drawn from European experience, including Franco-German reconciliation and the situation in Cyprus.

Good Friday Agreement:
Negotiation and Aftermath

—

The Good Friday Agreement: Why Then?

PADDY TEAHON

WHY DID IT TAKE FROM 1972 TO 1998 TO REACH THE GOOD FRIDAY AGREEMENT?

There was an important road from 1972 to 1998 through the Sunningdale conference, the Anglo-Irish Agreement and the Downing Street Agreement to the talks process that led to the Good Friday Agreement. During those years, it should be said, there were good relations between the Irish and British governments and between the various prime ministers and taoisigh. There were, in my view, two particular reasons for the 26-year intervening period from 1972 to 1998, namely:

- violence by the IRA and loyalist paramilitaries that exacerbated poor relations between the unionist and nationalist communities and their leaders;
- how successive UK governments understood the Northern Ireland question, and the impact of parliamentary arithmetic in Westminster.

The violence that marred life in Northern Ireland clearly meant that relations between nationalists and unionists were hugely negatively impacted. More than anything, the need to end violence and deliver peace for all the people on this island was what inspired all who saw themselves as being involved constructively in the peace process.

As the earlier chapters in this book show, there was extensive contact between various people—political leaders, advisers and civil servants, in Britain and Ireland, together with the involvement and support of US politicians and advisers—over several decades to establish a greater common awareness of the dimensions of the Northern Ireland Troubles, and explore ways of securing peace and reconciliation. This came together in the years leading up to 1998 with a group of people who had lived through almost 30 years of daily violence and deaths and were informed by their belief in the overriding value of peace, and a knowledge of Northern Ireland—the ideologies, aspirations and concerns of unionists and nationalists. I believe that values, relationships and trust developed over the years before 1998 encompass a great deal of what led to the Good Friday Agreement. The central or core value was peace and an end to violence. In many ways it linked to the other significant value of agreement, often phrased as 'nothing is agreed until everything is agreed'.

Relationships in my experience can develop from and relate strongly to values, and this was very true for the Irish peace process. Relationships at the political level and at the civil servant/political adviser level were critical in the negotiations that led to the Good Friday Agreement.

At the political level the closeness of the relationships between Bertie Ahern, who became taoiseach in 1997, Tony Blair, who became British prime minister also in 1997, and Bill Clinton, president of the United States (1992–2000) were, I am convinced, unique in the history of the three countries. The three men were elected to high office around the same time; they were of a similar age; and they were committed to a fresh approach to the Northern Ireland conflict. All three were convinced of the value of ending violence and were prepared to commit the time necessary to achieve that objective.

Their closeness flowed to and informed the relationships at the political adviser/civil servant level. There were Senator George Mitchell, Jim Steinberg and Sandy Berger from the US; John

Holmes and Jonathan Powell from the UK. On the Irish side, Tim Dalton, Dermot Gallagher (who, sadly, is no longer with us), Martin Mansergh, Sean O hUiginn and Tim O'Connor were a group of people that I was privileged to work with in the years that led up to April 1998. Many others were involved at different levels, including some of those who have contributed to this publication.

Civil servants from the Department of the Taoiseach, the Department of Foreign Affairs and the Department of Justice were involved directly in dealing with the peace process. Coming from different departments, we brought different perspectives to our work and that, I believe, was important given the nature of the issues involved. On occasion we did not start in agreement, but in my experience, because fundamentally we all wanted to achieve peace, we found our way to constructive agreement. The nature of most of the work meant that working in partnership was crucial, and was the working method that we used.

I want to acknowledge colleagues in the Department of the Taoiseach who worked on the peace process over many years. Dermot Nally, sadly no longer with us, has been recognised widely as having made a major contribution in Northern Ireland affairs over twenty years from 1972, when Jack Lynch brought him to the taoiseach's department. I never worked directly for Dermot but always enjoyed listening, mainly after golf games that we both enjoyed, to his many stories of events and personalities in his dealing with the peace process. Wally Kirwan, who did work directly with Dermot Nally, contributed over many years and was a valuable source of advice to me in the years from 1994 to 2000. Frank Murray, who succeeded Dermot Nally as secretary general to the government, was a great help to me in taking on responsibilities in the operation of the department when I was involved full-time in the peace process. That was true also for Dermot McCarthy, who succeeded Frank, and who was always ready to take on issues that would normally have been my responsibility. Frank Murray made a valuable contribution, after he retired, in working as co-commissioner on the Independent Commission for the Location of Victims' Remains, work that involved establishing where victims 'disappeared' by the IRA were buried, right up to the time he passed away in March 2018.

Returning to values, relationships and trust, in my view developed and dependable trust is built on shared values and close relationships. In the case of the peace process, the level of trust that came into being among the people I have identified made possible an effective negotiation process, which was critical where a complex series of elements had to be brought to a successful conclusion, ultimately in a very short period of time.

PERSONAL INVOLVEMENT IN THE PEACE PROCESS

There were many individuals that I related to over the years from 1993, when I became secretary general of the Department of the Taoiseach.

In the early part of that period, I believe the taoiseach, Albert Reynolds, deserves special mention. His work in what led to the IRA ceasefire of 1994 was a major achievement. I had a minor involvement but one that I believe is worth recalling, because it identifies the determination shown by Albert Reynolds as taoiseach.

In the lead-up to the 1994 ceasefire, the IRA was, as I understood it, offering a time-limited ceasefire of some six months' duration. One morning I received a phone call from Dick Spring, then tánaiste, who asked me to speak to the taoiseach and attempt to persuade him effectively to accept the six-month period. I went to see the taoiseach somewhat nervously, since I did not then deal with the peace process. Albert Reynolds was, as ever, totally direct, and on my asking what we would do, he said 'Paddy, if I am the last person that believes I can get a permanent ceasefire, that is what I will work for.' That ended the discussion and I believe summed up the determination of Albert Reynolds when he was committed to what he saw as being in the best interests of Ireland.

My next interaction with the peace process came in the early days of John Bruton's period as taoiseach. He called me to his office one morning and told me he was to have a meeting with Gerry Adams. He then said he needed a person to come with him. I was a little surprised, and was even more surprised when the taoiseach said 'You come with me', whereupon I said 'But I do not deal with the peace process', only to hear 'But you understand negotiation.'

I suspect I didn't realise that those words were to change the next seven years of my life.

It is fair to say that John Bruton's decision came as a surprise not just to me but to my colleagues who were already dealing with the peace process. I was fortunate that one of those colleagues was Tim Dalton, who was then secretary general of the Department of Justice and had been a friend since our days of second-level education in St Brendan's College Killarney. To Tim fell the job of educating me in the many dimensions of the peace process.

What followed over a seven-year period was a series of meetings, together with preparation for them and reflection on the outcomes, initially in my case with Sinn Féin but over time with all the parties and individuals involved in the peace process. A significant number of those meetings involved Martin McGuinness, either one-to-one or as part of groups.

A recent book by Jude Collins has set down the views of many of those involved in the peace process on McGuinness. I like in particular what President Bill Clinton said: that Martin McGuinness would give as his own eulogy 'I fought, I made peace, and I made politics.' Senator George Mitchell has an equivalent view: 'Martin certainly was a dominant figure in each phase: the phase of protest, the phase of negotiation and the phase of governance.' Those remarks I believe sum up a life that was a key part of realising peace by finding an end to violence. In dealing with Martin McGuinness you were conscious of his past, but I am convinced he was a person who came to recognise the value of peace, in particular for future generations, and the need to end violence to reach that objective.

In the early years of my involvement, Dermot Gleeson, then Ireland's attorney general, was a staunch colleague in our efforts during the time John Bruton was taoiseach, especially when the talks process commenced in Castle Buildings (Stormont). I have mentioned the group of civil servants/political advisers across the three countries—the UK, the USA and Ireland—whom it was my pleasure to work with over the years from 1993 to 2000. Not that we always agreed: in fact, one of the strengths of the relationships was that we could disagree constructively in the interest of finding the best way to peace.

A particular relationship is worth a special mention because of its link to the USA. This was with David Lavery, later chief of staff to David Trimble when the latter became first minister of Northern Ireland. David Lavery and I both became Eisenhower Fellows at an earlier stage of our careers. This fellowship programme, founded in Philadelphia in 1953 to honour US President Eisenhower in promoting the values of peace and prosperity, brought fourteen individuals—seven from Northern Ireland and seven from the south—to spend some months in the USA in 1989, visiting significant American leaders who were relevant to our careers. A particular focus of the programme was to promote interaction between people north and south, who would otherwise not have contact, about the Troubles in Northern Ireland and in what became the peace process; about how this interaction impacted on the lives of the visitors; and also, in time, about the role the USA might play in the process. David Lavery and I formed a special bond from our time in the USA that endures to the present day, and this effective back-channel proved valuable in the course of our involvement in the peace process. I believe the episode and the continuing commitment of the Eisenhower fellowships to Irish affairs demonstrate the international support for the lasting value of the Good Friday Agreement.

A feature of the intensity of the involvement of many people in the peace process is the impact on their families. Because I believe my own experience is representative of many others, I will recall it. The reality was that I spent many days and sometimes weeks away from home and from my wife Mary, my daughters Caroline and Marion and my son John. On occasion, on my return home, Marion opened the door of our house and told me with the good-natured sarcasm of a teenager that I showed good intelligence in finding the house given how seldom I got there.

In a short chapter such as this it is not feasible to recount very many of the events of the seven years from 1993 to 2000 that I was able to play a part in. Others have written at length of those years, not least Alastair Campbell in his extensive diaries, in which I feature from time to time.

What I will do is recall a specific event that I believe sums up the intensity of being involved in what led to the Good Friday

Agreement, and that has not, to my knowledge, been set down in detail elsewhere. In my view it provides an illustration of how the combination of shared values, close relationships and developed trust worked together at a vital stage.

That stage was reached on Holy Thursday and Good Friday, 9 and 10 April, 1998. The judgement of the two governments then on the likelihood of reaching agreement was not positive. There were indications that the UUP and the SDLP were making some progress, but Sinn Féin was suggesting it would not be part of an agreement.

At a point on Holy Thursday evening, the taoiseach, Bertie Ahern, called the key Irish officials together and said he was going to sit down with Martin McGuinness and Gerry Adams and would not allow them to leave the room until a deal had been reached. Adams and McGuiness accepted but produced a list of 78 issues they wished to discuss, which covered a wide range of matters that had arisen in the course of the negotiation. The taoiseach asked us officials to give him suggested answers to the issues. The essential point was to show that the two governments were prepared to identify clearly the progress that had been achieved and that could be incorporated into an agreement. Relationships and trust were called into play and draft answers were produced.

I was sent to ask Tony Blair to have Mo Mowlam join the taoiseach. Close relationships were again called upon. Mo was not convinced, and in her best colourful language let me have her views on the request, but in her equally genuine spirit came to join the negotiation, which went on for many hours into early Good Friday morning.

I want to take the opportunity to remember fondly my interactions with Mo Mowlam. She was a person who was motivated by the best instincts for what needed to be done, even where that cost her personally. The peace process would not have been the same without her.

Returning to that fateful night of Holy Thursday, trust was required in large measure in convincing our UK colleagues and, importantly, George Mitchell that there would be a successful outcome to the discussions with the Sinn Féin leaders. At a key moment early on Good Friday morning, Bill Clinton called Adams and McGuinness to underline the importance of reaching agreement and achieving peace.

The reality was that in those early hours we were not sure where Sinn Féin stood. Tension was high and lack of sleep played its part. Then, to our combined relief, Mitchel McLaughlin went out and briefed the media that Sinn Féin believed an agreement was possible.

As the two governments absorbed this crucial advance, the focus turned to the UUP. They had reached agreement with the SDLP on strand 1 issues, in particular the assembly, but now their attention turned to the specifics of the Sinn Féin accommodation—in particular to the issues of prisoners and of decommissioning.

Over a few hours, through the combined efforts of the two governments and thoughtful drafting, in particular by George Mitchell, we arrived at a plenary meeting with the agreed document 'Agreement reached in the multi-party negotiations'. I believe that the combination of shared values, close relationships and developed trust in a group of people—politicians, political advisers and official players—determined to achieve peace were remarkable.

WHAT NOW?

The core issue of this section is the relevance of the Good Friday Agreement in the world of 2018 and beyond. We live in particularly uncertain times in the island of Ireland, in our relationships with the UK and the EU and in terms of events right across the globe.

I believe that it is worthwhile to consider the following issues:

- the events since 1998, which, despite further bumps on the road, show the resilience of the Good Friday Agreement
- the Brexit situation, which underlines the importance of the agreement, in particular in the negotiation stance of the EU
- the need for debate in the context of the UK leaving the EU
- the importance of communities going forward.

The period from 1998 to 2007 was marked by negotiations to achieve arms decommissioning and by the coming together of the

DUP and Sinn Féin into the Northern Ireland executive. I believe that the events of that period underline the resilience of the Good Friday Agreement. It provided the foundation on which interactions took place and against which outcomes could be judged. That resilience was, I believe, a key factor in achieving, ultimately, the coming together of Sinn Féin and the DUP in an executive—a development that if mentioned in 1998 would have led many if not all to say 'impossible'. The events of this period have been set down comprehensively in a recent book by Mr Justice Richard Humphreys (*Beyond the border*), rightly described by Bertie Ahern as an essential read.

Those who suggest that the agreement has somehow outlived its usefulness do not in my view have the best interests of the island of Ireland, or indeed of the UK, at heart. In this context I particularly welcome what Jonathan Powell has had to say (in an article published by Queen's University):

> In any case, whatever the critics say, the British government is not about to walk away from the Good Friday Agreement. It is a legally binding treaty registered at the UN ... The Good Friday Agreement will survive for another twenty years as it has for the last twenty years. And we are right to celebrate the peace it has brought Northern Ireland in that time and will, I hope, continue to do in the future.

I agree strongly with Jonathan Powell's assessment. I believe we have underestimated the transformative impact of the lengthy period of sustained peace that the agreement has brought about. I also believe we need to redouble our commitment to maintaining that peace no matter what—that that goal trumps all others and will help us ultimately overcome all difficulties, both still existing (for example, the legacy of the past) and new ones that may arise in the future.

Brexit is clearly a most unwelcome development in the context of the Good Friday Agreement. The events that have surrounded the negotiations between the EU and the UK have been significantly contentious. Notwithstanding that, there is now (mid-November 2018) a draft withdrawal agreement. It contains a lengthy Protocol—'Ireland and Northern Ireland'—that includes the following:

AFFIRMING that the Good Friday or Belfast Agreement of 10 April 1998 between the Government of the United Kingdom, the Government of Ireland and the other participants in the multi-party negotiations (the '1998 Agreement'), which is annexed to the British–Irish Agreement of the same date (the 'British–Irish Agreement'), including its subsequent implementation agreements and arrangements, should be protected in all its parts.

This I believe is a most welcome and important statement. Only time will tell if the draft can be turned into reality. What I feel is worth underlining is the importance of the Good Friday Agreement in the negotiating stance of the EU. Without it I wonder what would have emerged.

The impact of the UK leaving the EU creates major and unprecedented issues for Ireland, for the EU and for the UK. It is unclear even now when an outcome will emerge. The reality is that if Brexit takes place, the UK will no longer be a member of the EU. For Ireland south and north it is a time when I believe thought should be given to how best to deal with that change.

One element that I suggest deserves special attention is the role and place of communities. It is at the local level that much needs to be done and much can be achieved. People on the ground in communities understand better than anybody that there can be no going back to the horrors of the past, the price for which was paid on their streets and in their homes, and that peace remains the only path forward.

CONCLUSION

I hope I have conveyed in this chapter what a memorable personal experience it was to have been able to play a part in the peace process. I also hope that offering an understanding of what led to the Good Friday Agreement and what it means today can be useful in valuing what was achieved and showing why it should be treasured for the years to come.

My Journey to the Good Friday Agreement

DAVID DONOGHUE

My own journey towards the Good Friday Agreement began in the mid-1970s, when as a young third secretary I joined what was then a tiny Anglo-Irish section in the Department of Foreign Affairs under Seán Donlon. It was a period of deep confrontation and near-despair in the north, characterised by a sharply deteriorating security situation and, in the wake of the collapse of the power-sharing executive in 1974, an ominous political vacuum. I spent a year working in the section. Among my responsibilities—and it is a sign of how bleak the situation was at that time—was helping to prepare a so-called 'Doomsday plan' to cater for the implications in the south of a widely anticipated breakdown of law and order in the north.

A decade later I found myself back in the Anglo-Irish section, as part of a not much bigger team under the leadership of Michael Lillis. On this occasion, there was a much more promising, indeed a momentous, agenda. The government was in the final stages of negotiations with the British government on what would become the Anglo-Irish Agreement. This had the potential to transform the prospects for political progress in Northern Ireland. It would bring us for the first time into a serious policy engagement with the British in relation to Northern Ireland. It would launch a genuine partnership between the two governments that would lay the basis for the peace process over the following decade—and, indeed, without which there was no chance of that peace process succeeding.

I was part of the Dublin team that supported the newly established Anglo-Irish secretariat in Belfast. Declan O'Donovan and I and other colleagues worked on the broad range of issues covering security policy, human-rights concerns and the administration of justice in Northern Ireland. We had to ensure that our colleagues in the secretariat, or the 'Bunker' as it was nicknamed, would have the best possible material to work from in presenting 'views and proposals' on these subjects to their British counterparts. This meant assembling the best possible picture of what was happening on the ground and developing in compelling detail the case for policy reforms. One of the tools we used was a comprehensive network of local contacts that we built up in the first years of the agreement. I was assigned at an early stage to this contact work.

My next posting was to the embassy in London as press officer covering the UK media. The focus of that work was almost exclusively on Northern Ireland and Anglo-Irish relations. These relations were under some strain at the time (the late 1980s) because of a succession of security and legal controversies that divided the Irish and British governments, led respectively by Charles Haughey and Margaret Thatcher. But we managed to weather those storms. Even if the two governments differed on individual issues, the institutional arrangements established between them under the Anglo-Irish Agreement and otherwise provided a solid basis for dialogue, cooperation and—over time—a gradual narrowing of those differences.

In 1991 I returned to Dublin and rejoined what was now the Anglo-Irish division. I was effectively the deputy to Sean O hUiginn, who had just taken over as head of the division and who over the next few years would play a central role for the Irish government in the emerging peace process. These were challenging and difficult years as successive governments endeavoured to bring about an inclusive negotiation process that would provide a basis for the ending of all paramilitary campaigns and for the achievement of a comprehensive political settlement. It was a period of intense but ultimately rewarding activity. Landmark events included the Downing Street Declaration of December 1993, the IRA ceasefire of August 1994, the joint framework document of February 1995, the launching of three-stranded talks in June 1996, the restored IRA ceasefire of July 1997 and the achievement of the Good Friday Agreement in April 1998.

In 1995 I moved to Belfast to become the Irish head of the Anglo-Irish secretariat. I spent four years there, handling much of the day-to-day contact with British officials on the multiple challenges facing the peace process. I was closely involved in the negotiations, spread out over several years, which in April 1998 finally culminated in the Good Friday Agreement. Under an informal understanding reached in the margins of that agreement, the two governments decided to close the Maryfield secretariat (which was to be replaced by a new institution, the British–Irish secretariat). I was, accordingly, the last Irish joint secretary in Maryfield and I oversaw the transition to the new institution, and premises, before moving on to a new role abroad.

The direct personal engagement of successive taoisigh and ministers was a key factor in the success of the peace process during the 1990s. They provided critical political impetus and direction; they worked hard on their British counterparts to build a common view of how peace and a comprehensive political settlement might be secured; and they were willing to take risks in pursuit of those goals.

They were supported in their efforts by dedicated officials from a number of government departments. In the years leading to the Good Friday Agreement, the Irish government team for the negotiations included some of the finest talents in the Irish public service. The team benefited enormously from the leadership, strategic vision and tactical skills of Sean O hUiginn, the late Dermot Gallagher, Paddy Teahon and Tim Dalton. Outstanding contributions were also made during this period by David Cooney, Rory Montgomery, Tim O'Connor, Eamonn McKee, Ray Bassett, Wally Kirwan and several others, as well as by gifted political advisers such as Martin Mansergh, Seán Donlon and Fergus Finlay.

A concerted team effort on the Irish side, encompassing both the political and official levels, delivered the key achievements of the peace process. In the run-up to the Good Friday Agreement, Irish ministers (David Andrews and Liz O'Donnell) made significant contributions, interacting with British counterparts such as Mo Mowlam and Paul Murphy and with the Northern Ireland parties. The then attorney general, David Byrne, also played an important role.

We dealt with some very talented and astute British officials throughout the 1990s. The British team was drawn mainly from the Northern Ireland Office but included also some Foreign Office and Cabinet Office representation. The format generally used for work on joint documents and shared analysis of developments in the peace process was a so-called liaison group that met variously in London, Belfast or Dublin. In my time, this was led on the British side by Quentin Thomas and, from April 1998 onwards, by Bill Jeffrey. On the Irish side, it was led by Sean O hUiginn and, from the summer of 1997 onwards, by Dermot Gallagher.

There were, of course, additional formats and channels for contact at official level. In particular, there was very close contact between the taoiseach's department and the prime minister's office. But many of the key documents during the 1990s were negotiated and agreed through the mechanism of the liaison group. When negotiations involving the two governments and the parties got underway, the delegations of the two governments maintained continuous contact with each other through the liaison group in order to assess progress, to respond to crises in a coordinated fashion and to develop joint positions on issues of substance, procedure or tactics.

A colleague has made the point that, every now and then over the past three decades, the British government has had to re-learn the importance of its partnership with us. I very much agree. I would like to think, however, that during the 1990s the learning curve became a little bit less steep as we built up successive layers of agreement with each other. We did this through the painstaking negotiation of a series of joint documents or, in some instances, British government declarations on which we had been closely consulted in advance.

One such was a statement by Peter Brooke, the then Secretary of State for Northern Ireland, in March 1991. This made clear that the British government had no strategic or economic interest of its own in remaining in Northern Ireland and went on to open up the prospect of three-stranded talks aimed at a comprehensive political settlement. This was a particularly significant declaration of position by the British government, which helped to bring about the first round of three-stranded negotiations a year later. Even if these ran into the ground eventually and collapsed in the summer of 1992, there were at least some valuable exploratory exchanges, notably between the Irish government and the unionist parties in strand 2. The basic concept of a three-stranded settlement, underpinned by a balanced constitutional accommodation, was established.

Meanwhile, various informal contacts with the republican movement, including what became known as the Hume–Adams dialogue, led to a judgement on the part of both governments that there might now be an opportunity, if carefully managed, to bring about an end to the Provisional IRA campaign and the related loyalist paramilitary campaigns. Intensive work began on the preparation of a joint position by the two governments that would set out the parameters of an inclusive political process, involving as the condition of participation the complete abandonment of violence, and also the kind of settlement that the two governments considered would be attainable through this route. The result of this work, the Downing Street Declaration, was of pivotal importance in moving the peace process forward. Eight months later, the Provisional IRA announced a ceasefire.

The next major joint text was the joint framework document of February 1995. This was in effect a detailed prospectus for the future negotiations, setting out what the two governments felt could, indeed should, be agreed within the three strands and also providing their joint vision for the constitutional component of the future agreement, policing reform and all other key elements. It was an ambitious document, clearly signalling the broad scope and potential of the negotiation process that was envisaged and the acceptance by both governments of an entirely open-ended agenda.

Unfortunately, the issue of the decommissioning of paramilitary weapons moved increasingly centre-stage during 1995–6. This was in large measure because of the political dependence of the Major government on unionist MPs' support at Westminster and the government's consequent susceptibility to unionist pressure. The issue itself, presented by unionists as a precondition for the launching of inclusive negotiations, was viewed by us as an unnecessary impediment with the capacity to wreck the entire project. Entry to the talks and participation in them should be on the basis of the 'Mitchell principles' alone (the commitments to non-violence developed by Senator George Mitchell for this process). Everyone accepted that the issue of paramilitary weapons would have to be addressed as part of a comprehensive settlement. But to require that this be done before participants even reached the negotiating table was without precedent in other peace processes, and, if supported by the British government, stood a good chance of destroying ours.

Much political energy was expended by Irish ministers and officials on efforts to dissuade the British government from going down that road. Over time, we were successful as British ministers gradually modified their position. However, the decommissioning issue—which some saw as a deliberate delaying tactic on the part of unionists to forestall political engagement with republicans— weighed heavily over the process for many years. In the spring of 1996 the Canary Wharf bombing brought the IRA ceasefire to an abrupt halt; many attributed this to republican disillusionment with the slow pace of political progress due to the impasse over decommissioning. Talks got underway in June of that year, minus Sinn Féin. They were bedevilled, however, by protracted procedural wrangling, much of it traceable to unionist determination to ensure that, if Sinn Féin found itself back in the process courtesy of a renewed IRA ceasefire, no political progress would occur without some movement on decommissioning.

The Irish government worked intensively behind the scenes to create the conditions for a restoration of the ceasefire and inclusive talks. Alongside these efforts came the prospect of a change of government in each jurisdiction and a new political dynamic that that would bring. In the summer of 1997 administrations headed by Bertie Ahern and Tony Blair respectively took office in Dublin and London. Each of the new leaders could be described as pragmatic, lacking any kind of 'baggage' on the Northern Ireland issue and determined to give top priority to the pursuit of a comprehensive settlement. Each government had a comfortable majority. As Paddy Teahon has remarked, the new taoiseach and prime minister had exceptionally good personal chemistry and rapidly developed a close working relationship. On top of that came their partnership with President Bill Clinton, unique among US presidents in the degree of his interest in, and understanding of, the Northern Ireland problem as well as in his ability to win the trust of both communities. A further confidence-building factor was the continuing role played by George Mitchell, an inspired choice by President Clinton, who impressed all with his remarkable chairing skills and political acumen and who was trusted and respected on all sides.

In short, the stars were now well aligned—possibly better than they had ever been before. The combination of these factors, plus the intensive groundwork done by the Irish government over the preceding year, led in reasonably short order to the restoration of the IRA ceasefire. This cleared the way for Sinn Féin to join the talks. I remember vividly a huge sense of relief that summer that, after months and even years of procedural stalemate, we were now finally on the cusp of negotiations that would address the substance of a comprehensive settlement.

In the short term, of course, the DUP walked out and the UUP, taunted mercilessly by Ian Paisley and Robert McCartney, were under intense pressure to do likewise. To his great credit, David Trimble resisted this pressure and kept his party in. As he needed some political cover before resuming with Sinn Féin at the table, it was a month or two before the inclusive talks were finally launched (at the end of September 1997). For the UUP's decision to stay in, Trimble exacted a price: he and his colleagues would have no direct dialogue with Sinn Féin for the duration of the negotiations. While this was initially greeted with a certain amount of bemusement, after a while it began to inject tension into the negotiations. Beyond its immediate implications for UUP–Sinn Féin relations, there were wider ripples of tension with other parties over the UUP's treatment of a legitimate participant in the talks.

On a lighter note, I recall fondly an occasion when Gerry Adams dispensed with the procedure, insisted on by the UUP, of routing his comments to the UUP through the chair and tried to seduce David Trimble into a direct exchange across the room. Trimble was having none of it and stared grimly ahead. Adams later tried the same approach with John Taylor, now in the UUP seat, who winked back at the Sinn Féin leader as if to say 'Do you think I'm going to fall for that?' At that moment, the lights in the room went out—it transpired later, because of a technical fault. When they were restored a few minutes later, Taylor was gone. It was a surreal moment that, some quipped, might have been Glengall Street (location of the UUP headquarters) intervening rapidly to head off a premature move on Taylor's part towards direct dialogue with Sinn Féin.

The opening months in fact saw considerably less progress than we had hoped for. While negotiations were opened in all three stands, and a range of subsidiary bodies were set up, there was much 'grandstanding' and little real engagement. By Christmas a degree of disillusionment was setting in all round.

It fell to George Mitchell, and to the two governments, to try to inject momentum into the process. Senator Mitchell worked in various gentle ways to push things forward and to try to give the parties a sense of the overall prize that awaited them if the negotiations were to conclude successfully. Partly this involved helping them to see the contours of an overall agreement and the trade-offs and balances across the different strands. Of course, there were risks involved in this. In particular, there was a risk that the unionists would run scared if they were to see at too early a stage the full measure of what they might have to—or indeed would have to—agree to. But George Mitchell nudged the parties forward with his inimitable tact and patience, encouraging them towards a comprehensive view of the likely settlement and underlining the need for compromise across all three strands and in the other parts of the agreement.

The two governments, for their part, developed early in 1998 a so-called heads of agreement paper that sought to map out, as we saw them, the key elements of that agreement. Though obviously some parties highlighted particular parts of the paper and downplayed or ignored others in line with their own priorities, on the whole it made an important contribution by giving the talks badly needed focus and direction.

There was a marked stepping-up of pace and engagement from about February onwards. The two governments had signalled their view that the negotiations should conclude by Easter, so as to permit the referendums to be held in May (in advance of the marching season, which could be expected to be violent and disruptive). Senator Mitchell echoed this time-frame. In addition, at the beginning of Easter week he applied some gentle pressure to the participants relating to his own family circumstances and his absolute need to go home at Easter (with a strong hint that he might not be able to return). Such was the respect everyone had for the senator, and the personal sacrifices he had made, that this proved a very effective additional incentive to reach agreement before Easter.

To keep the momentum going, and for other tactical reasons, the talks were moved to London and Dublin for two sessions lasting several days each. In the event, the Dublin session was overshadowed by a bitter controversy over whether Sinn Féin should be expelled from the talks because of apparent republican involvement in two murders. Alleged breaches of the Mitchell principles by one or other party linked to paramilitary groups punctuated the negotiations at regular intervals. As they involved a fundamental condition of participation in the talks, and a procedure had to be invoked each time requiring immediate consideration of the alleged breach by the two governments, there was inevitably a loss of momentum in terms of the substantive negotiations. These interruptions could perhaps be described as a necessary evil. In this instance, Sinn Féin was temporarily expelled but returned to the table a fortnight later.

This brings us finally to Easter week.

It began with a pivotal moment: George Mitchell's tabling of a paper that he presented as his best assessment of where agreement might be found. Prepared in the closest consultation with the two governments, this laid out with greater precision and comprehensiveness than anything previously attempted the likely content of the agreement we were hoping to achieve by the end of that week. It followed very closely the terms of the framework document. While the British government in private contacts with the unionists would occasionally resile from the framework document, in public comments it remained largely committed to it.

The next pivotal moment was the arrival of the taoiseach and the prime minister at the talks—a calculated signal to all participants that we were now in the end game.

The Mitchell paper was dismissed immediately by the unionists for its treatment of Strand 2 issues, John Taylor famously pronouncing that he would not touch it 'with a 40-foot barge pole'. But negotiations based on it were nevertheless underway with the unionists within 24 hours. We insisted to the British government that there could be no dilution of the basic position that the north–south ministerial council and the implementation bodies would be protected from abuse by a unionist majority in the assembly. With that principle firmly established, we were prepared to row back somewhat on the number and choice of functional areas for the implementation bodies. This was a necessary rebalancing. I recall Bertie Ahern saying at the time that 'everyone has to be a winner'; with that in mind, we felt we had to show some flexibility on the functions for the bodies (which could of course be added to over time) in exchange for getting the right basis for the north–south machinery from the outset.

When Strand 2 was finally agreed in the late evening of Holy Thursday, that cleared the way for surprisingly rapid agreement on Strand 1. The key players here were the UUP and the SDLP; Sinn Féin's lack of interest in Strand 1 had been obvious throughout the negotiations and it, like others, was a little taken aback by the speed with which agreement was reached there once the basic deal had been done in Strand 2.

There were several more moments of drama to come. I remember everyone struggling to wake up as Good Friday dawned: exhausted after a night spent trying to grab some sleep on top of, or under, desks or tables but at the same time warily realising that agreement might perhaps just be at hand. Then, as the morning wore on, we began to hear of the internal difficulties in the UUP delegation over prisoner releases and decommissioning. I remember concluding gloomily with a colleague over lunchtime that the agreement that had seemed so close would now evaporate and that it could be years before we would be able to rebuild things to that point. And then, to our amazement, George Mitchell rang us in the late afternoon to say that David Trimble had just told him that he was ready to sign up. The plenary meeting a few minutes later, with assent conveyed in the clearest terms by each delegation leader, was an extraordinary moment that I will never forget.

The Good Friday Agreement, overwhelmingly endorsed by the people of Ireland a couple of months later, has been through many testing times since then. With continuing sharp disagreements over decommissioning, years were to go by before the institutions it had established were fully up and running. And today we are dealing with another prolonged and damaging hiatus.

But it is still a unique achievement by international standards. Even if it has failed to end sectarianism or to deliver social reform on the scale hoped for, it continues to ensure lasting peace and stability in Northern Ireland. It is looked to internationally as one of the very few examples in the world today of successful conflict resolution. And it is fair to say that, in its key principles and the institutions it has created, the agreement closely reflects the consistent analysis by successive Irish governments of how best to build a lasting accommodation between the two main traditions on the island.

North–South Cooperation and the Good Friday Agreement: a Story of Good Architecture

TIM O'CONNOR

I am concentrating in my contribution on a particular dimension of the Good Friday Agreement—Strand 2, the new north–south arrangements. Just for the record, I was part of the Irish government negotiating team in the multi-party talks that led to the agreement, working with several others under the direction of Dermot Gallagher in the Anglo-Irish division of the Department of Foreign Affairs, in support of the taoiseach and the ministers involved.

I had begun working in the Anglo-Irish division in 1986, when I started a four-year stint, returning as a counsellor in 1994, where my role was preparing for and eventually working on the Forum for Peace and Reconciliation. After the breakdown of the IRA ceasefire in February 1996 the forum was suspended and I was transferred out of the Anglo-Irish division, serving as Africa director for the 1996 presidency of the EU and as director of the human rights unit for a period in 1997. In October 1997 Dermot Gallagher asked me to return to the Anglo-Irish division and I remained working on Northern Ireland for the next eight years: first on the talks team, subsequently on the setting up the north/south structures, and ultimately, on promotion to assistant secretary general in 1999, as the first southern head of the north–south ministerial council joint secretariat based in Armagh, a post I held until 2005.

Dermot Gallagher was a giant of the peace process and somebody hugely special in the lives and careers of many of the contributors to this book. I will never forget the immense work done in tandem in the lead-up to Good Friday 1998 by Dermot, Paddy Teahon and Tim Dalton, as the three lead officials on the Irish government team. I salute all the colleagues who were involved in the peace process over previous years, those others who served in the agreement years and since then, and those who hold the fort now, led by Fergal Mythen. We all share the privilege of working or having worked in our careers on the single most important issue of our time, the creation of a sustained peace on our island.

I have just finished reading Noel Dorr's superb book on Sunningdale, which brought home to us all again just how problematic the north–south relationship was in the overall scheme of things. Indeed, in 1998, we experienced how chill its wind could be right up to the wire on Good Friday. It is a matter of public record that when George Mitchell circulated the first outline of a draft agreement on Monday, 6 April 1998—four days before ultimate success—the north–south section , which was quite elaborate, was a key reason why the overall draft agreement was rejected out of hand by the UUP, with deputy leader John Taylor saying he wouldn't touch it with a 40-foot barge pole!

In the following days, the north–south section had to be very significantly recast and a new approach was developed whereby only the framework and principles of a new accommodation on north–south relations would be contained in the agreement, with negotiations on the detail to follow afterwards. That shift contributed significantly to the breakthrough on Good Friday and the conclusion of a comprehensive agreement.

Once the agreement had been approved by the people of Ireland north and south in the simultaneous referenda on 22 May 1998, the way was clear for the negotiations to begin on the detail of a new north–south dispensation. In a sense this was an entirely new talks process, though of course we did have the wind of the agreement behind us. Dermot Gallagher asked me to head up the Department of Foreign Affairs team on those talks and I was ably assisted by Rory Montgomery and James McIntyre, and later by Helena Nolan. We worked closely with Paddy Teahon in the taoiseach's department and his team led by Wally Kirwan.

In brief summary, over the next ten months we were engaged with the Northern Ireland Office and the Northern Ireland parties in an intensive process of negotiation —first to identify the twelve areas that would constitute the substance of the work of the north–south Ministerial Council (NSMC), and then to put flesh on their bones. Six were to be implemented by existing bodies north and south and six by dint of new implementation bodies to be created on an all-island basis. It took a long time but we got there, and on 8 March 1999 a new international agreement establishing the cross-border bodies was signed by Secretary of State for Northern Ireland Mo Mowlam and Minister for Foreign Affairs David Andrews. I wish to record here my appreciation of the good working relations we enjoyed with our Northern Ireland civil service partners during this process, the latter ably led by Tony McCusker and Rosalie Flanagan, supported by Denis McCartney and others.

Noel Dorr's book notes that there were different views in 1973–4 as to how committed the Irish civil service was to embracing cross-border cooperation. I can safely assert that in 1998–9 we had a different experience. There was extensive buy-in by departments and the process of establishing and taking forward the bodies involved a huge quantum of work by a large cohort of colleagues all around the civil service, which we all greatly appreciated.

The task involved in respect of the cross-border bodies was intense and complex. In essence what we were doing was building an entirely new dispensation of public administration on the island of Ireland —the most profound change in that regard since the setting up of the two administrations in Ireland in the early 1920s. Apart from the political sensitivities involved, there were major technical and administrative challenges. After 70 years the two systems of public administration, which had common origins in the British administration in Ireland under the Union, had, in many instances, evolved in very different ways.

But we got there, and the cross-border bodies came into being with the other institutions on 2 December 1999. Today over 1,000 people are employed in these cross-border bodies, doing great work across a wide range of areas. Cross-border cooperation has been one of the quiet success stories of the Good Friday Agreement.

How did that happen when we contrast the different experience at Sunningdale? David Trimble has an interesting suggestion in terms of the answer —on Good Friday, he suggested, 'we got the architecture right' on north–south relations, meaning the design, the compromises, the checks and balances.

Just a brief word on what that meant in practice. First, in the design of the overall north–south package itself in the Good Friday Agreement, a careful balance was struck. The Irish government and nationalist parties got their wish in terms of having an institutional expression of the relationship between the two parts of Ireland in the form of the north–south ministerial council and (ultimately) the seven new cross-border bodies. On the other hand, the unionist parties got their wish in ensuring that (a) the scope of what was covered in the new dispensation was much more modest than the original wish-list of the Irish government and nationalists and (b) careful checks and balances were built into the operating model of the north–south ministerial council and the cross-border bodies so that in effect unionist ministers in the north had a veto over every decision.

One example of those checks and balances in operation was the fact that at all sectoral meetings of the NSMC (when, say, the Irish minister for education was meeting a northern counterpart), the Northern Ireland minister was always accompanied by a minister from the other tradition, even though the latter had nothing to do with the substance of that area. So, for instance, when Martin McGuinness, the Northern Ireland education minister, was meeting his counterpart Michael Woods in the education sectoral NSMC, he (McGuinness) was always accompanied by a unionist minister. In addition, all decisions of the NSMC had to be by unanimous agreement—meaning that if the unionist minister disagreed, no decision could be taken.

All this sounds cumbersome, but we strove hard to make it work. And it did. For the first five-and-a-half years of the life of the NSMC (December 1999 to summer 2005), I was, as mentioned, its southern joint secretary and I worked on all of this at first hand. The joint secretariat of the NSMC was based in Armagh and comprised about 30 officials, roughly half from the Northern Ireland civil service and half from the Irish civil service. Some three years before I had been Africa director for Ireland's presidency of the EU in 1996, and I served as chairman of the EU Africa Working Group during that period. We met monthly in Brussels and prepared the Africa material for the EU Foreign Affairs Council meetings. That gave me a bird's-eye view of how that council system worked, and I suggested we follow that (tried and trusted) example closely in developing the working model of the NSMC. This was readily agreed to by the Northern Ireland side and that system of careful preparation of meetings—using the working group model, which I and my Northern Ireland counterpart co-chaired—worked very well in building confidence, especially in the early period. We also sought to ensure that the meetings of ministers went as smoothly as possible. In particular, we sought to operate the principle of 'no surprises'. Meetings proceeded as we said they would and we paid careful attention to the practical arrangements so that everybody could operate comfortably. Within months, things settled down and, broadly speaking, the NSMC worked very calmly and well.

In the period between December 1999 and the suspension of the Northern Ireland institutions in October 2002, there were 65 meetings of the north–south ministerial council in its different formats. That meant 65 meetings of ministers from north and south, all passing off efficiently and smoothly with a huge amount of quiet work being approved and moved on. Contrast that with the previous 75 years—and in particular the situation at Sunningdale, where it wasn't even possible to get agreement on what the Council of Ireland would look like.

Meanwhile, and in parallel, the work of setting up and moving forward with the cross-border bodies proceeded efficiently and effectively, under the direction of the NSMC. Certainly, as mentioned, the work involved was complex, but the mood and tone were solutions-focused and on all issues we found a way. For all of us involved, it was a very special time, and I want to use this opportunity to pay tribute to my colleagues north and south in the joint secretariat in Armagh during those years. It was one of the most uplifting projects of my career and a hugely positive professional and indeed personal experience.

Gradually, and actually quite quickly, therefore, the heat went out of the north–south issue, and what had been a hugely contentious and divisive topic right up to the week of the Good Friday Agreement itself became almost a matter of routine within months after the agreement's coming into operation. Much of the credit for that goes to David Trimble's point about getting the architecture right.

I want to close by highlighting the achievements of just one of the cross-border bodies, Tourism Ireland.

Like a smiling parent, I am particularly proud of the work of Tourism Ireland, and it bothers me that people seem to forget that it is a direct child of the Good Friday Agreement! It was formally brought into being at an NSMC meeting in late 2000. Under excellent boards and two great CEOs, first Paul O'Toole and now Niall Gibbons, Tourism Ireland has done a spectacular job in marketing and promoting the entire island of Ireland around the world as a world-class tourism destination.

Just take a look at some key facts and figures.

- Projected number of international visitors to the island in 2018: 10.8 million; that number in 2002, as Tourism Ireland was getting going, was 7 million—a 54% increase in the interim.
- Spend by those visitors today: €6 billion.
- Number of people working in the tourism sector north and south: 280,000.
- Tourism is the fastest growing source of employment in Northern Ireland.
- There are currently 2,000 hotel beds under construction in Belfast, representing a 25% increase in capacity.
- The *Lonely Planet Guide* voted Belfast and the Causeway Coastal Route the number 1 destination globally to visit in 2018.
- And finally, a remarkable fact: 30 years ago the Giant's Causeway had 100,000 visitors per year. In 2017 it welcomed one million!

That is one answer to those who say that the Good Friday Agreement is dying or has failed.

And there is another answer to the talk of failure. The biggest dividend of the Good Friday Agreement is that it has brought us twenty years of sustained peace on our island. Each year that passes, a bit like the EU and peace in Europe, makes it hopefully more and more unthinkable that we would ever go back to the darkness that we ended on 10 April 1998. If you have forgotten what that darkness felt like, take a look at the BBC documentary *The funeral murders*, aired in March 2018, or Gerry Moriarty's article in *The Irish Times* on the same day, recalling the same tragic events of 1988. Certainly, there is a lot more work to be done, but the foundations on which to build that work are solid and strong.

A good American friend of mine, Dr Jack Cochran, has taught me the maxim that our primary responsibility as human beings is to be good ancestors. My hope is that history will show that the Good Friday Agreement proved to be a major act of good ancestry, and now our task is to continue to build on its platform. That work goes on.

Two Inspectors Call … and Other Events

TIM DALTON

The term 'Irish peace process' conjures up a wide variety of images. For many television viewers, one image is that of lines of black limousines proceeding in convoy towards great media-clad castles and mansions where they decanted dark-suited men of serious mien who promptly disappeared indoors, there to joust intellectually, often for days and nights on end, in an effort to bring the Northern Ireland Troubles to an end.

Not all the decantees were men, of course. Some well-known women were inside the railings also, participated fully in the fray, and made a valuable contribution to the various declarations and agreements that, cumulatively and over a period that began long before the 1990s, saw the years of misery, destruction and death on this island consigned in virtually all but memory to the past.

These gatherings were essential to the success of the peace process but, as all those who were closer to the process will know, they don't tell the whole story. Countless meetings took place both before and after the 'castle' gatherings, where small teams of Irish and British civil servants—sometimes accompanied by ministers, sometimes not—engaged with one another, away from the limelight, at various venues and at all hours, trying to pull together the thoughts and the documents that would set the agenda for the greater gatherings and form a basis for making progress.

I had the privilege, as secretary general of the Department of Justice and Equality in the years 1993 to 2004, of playing a part in all of this. What I have to say is based on that experience.

On the Irish side, three government departments played a more frontline role than did other departments in advancing the peace process—the taoiseach's department, foreign affairs and justice. The lead civil service team on the Irish side comprised the secretaries general of those three departments (in the case of foreign affairs, sometimes the head of the Anglo-Irish division played the lead role). In my time, these three officials, along with Dr Martin Mansergh, were referred to jokingly by colleagues as the Four Horsemen (not to be confused with the real and earlier team of that name—leading US politicians Tip O'Neill, Ted Kennedy, Daniel P. Moynihan and Hugh Carey).

This team was supported by a number of other civil servants, most of whom were drawn from the Department of Foreign Affairs. Many of those involved are well known and some have contributed to this publication. Sadly, there are others who played a very significant part during those years but are no longer with us, including the late Dermot Gallagher, with whom I spent many hours working—and sometimes relaxing—at various venues in Belfast, Derry, London, Dublin and, indeed, Crossmaglen.

The number of Department of Justice people involved was relatively small. Ken O'Leary, who was assistant secretary with responsibility for matters to do with Northern Ireland and national security, accompanied me to most gatherings; not only those attended by leading political figures but also to the low-key, unpublicised meetings where he and I—sometimes accompanied by other Irish and British officials, sometimes on our own—met with senior Sinn Féin figures, trying to identify hitherto unexplored pathways that might lead us all closer to a lasting peace.

These side meetings, in my view, made an important contribution to the overall success of the peace process. They afforded us the opportunity of raising issues and floating ideas that could not be raised as easily in more formal settings. They also provided an opportunity for getting to know the people we were dealing with, enabled us to talk about important matters other than peace-making (such as the qualities and likely fortunes of Gaelic football teams) and generally get a sense of what motivated people. As anybody who has engaged in negotiations of any kind will appreciate, it is important to get to know the people at the other side of the table and try to understand why they see the world in a way that is very different from the view through your own eyes. I have no doubt that the same was true on the other side of the table; they too were working out what we were 'like' as individuals and whether we were people who could be trusted.

These informal meetings were not risk-free. Running through all engagements was an understandable effort to find out what was the most that might be offered, or the least that might be accepted by the other side. There was always the risk, for a government official, of overstepping the mark in assessing what might be offered or accepted by governments. There was no possibility of checking back with ministers at every hand's turn, there is no convenient handbook that covers such situations and there was no room either for taking 'flyers'. It was a case of using best judgement, entering all the necessary caveats and ensuring that the caveats were understood and were fully absorbed. 'What if?', in other words, was always a question, never a promise.

Life had been so different in doing our usual job of trying to ensure that persons involved in paramilitary organisations were charged, convicted and imprisoned. Trying to bring paramilitary activities, and all that surrounded them, to an end was a very different challenge. Indeed, the question can be asked as to how a Department of Justice, given its role and responsibilities, could engage with people who might be seen as the antithesis of what the department represented. The reality, though, was that there was a chance that persisting with talks could bring the troubles on this island to an end. Whatever the Department of Justice could do to help that process we were going to do.

Documents produced along the way by officials on both sides were shared—often very sparingly, and often carrying a 'secret' classification. There was an ongoing concern that papers still in the course of evolution would find their way to the media and into the wider political arena before they were introduced at the talks table. Parts of the documents that might be particularly challenging for one side or another might be quoted selectively and out of context, thus forcing a political party to deliver a public response from which they might find it impossible later to resile, even if they might wish to take a different line on seeing the full document and listening to the reasoning of its authors.

While draft documents were shared among the lead team members—and often more widely within the teams—and it was open to all of us to contribute to discussions on those documents, there was an understanding and expectation that some of us would pay particular attention to specific topics. The justice team was expected to take a particular interest in security issues: such as attempting to assess the likely attitude of the IRA to various proposals under consideration. This was a subset of what we thought was the IRA's current attitude towards peace-making generally. For example, was the search for an exclusively peaceful way forward a genuine IRA objective or simply a strategy to secure a badly needed break for war-weary activists?

Other topics that were clearly within the remit of the justice team were arms decommissioning, prisoners, policing and—at a later time—normalisation/demilitarisation, how to deal with the so-called 'on the runs' (OTRs) and the 'disappeared'. None of these topics were reserved exclusively for justice personnel. All three departmental teams brought their expertise on all issues to the table, as did our British counterparts. Without that mix of input, progress would not have been possible and without the political leadership of the taoiseach and the prime minister, together with their ministers, the desired results would not have been delivered.

Attempting to determine the likely attitude of the IRA at particular points or their likely reactions to proposals being developed at political level was not an exact science. In order to make a reasonable fist of it, Ken and I met on a very regular basis with the commissioner of An Garda Síochána and his senior team on the security side. At these meetings we briefed the gardaí on what was happening at the negotiating table and on what was emerging in other conversations we were part of. They in turn briefed us on what they saw happening on the ground. Our constant engagement with the gardaí was no dark secret—Sinn Féin would have known that it was part of my job to stay in touch with the gardaí about these matters and I would have said to Sinn Féin representatives, at times, that information coming from the gardaí was troubling in so far as progress towards peace was concerned. Apart from being able to check whether any euphoria (or its opposite) that might be emerging at the talks table was matched by the observed reality on the ground, these meetings enabled us to convey some messages to the gardaí that were important in terms of spreading the peace message within the republican family.

On more than one occasion, one of the senior Sinn Féin representatives said to us that meetings being organised by Sinn Féin to keep the organisation's grassroots up to speed with progress on the political front were being disrupted due to excessive Garda surveillance (or 'harassment' as it was described). This, we were told, made the task of advancing towards an exclusively peaceful strategy slower and more difficult than it needed to be. The gardaí, over many years, naturally kept an eye on republican gatherings—two or more eyes, in fact, when very senior players were in attendance. That was part of their job. We couldn't, now, tell them to 'ease up' on the basis that some of the meetings had a benign purpose, that is, to enable leaders who were pro-peace to explain to grassroots supporters that the political negotiations were pushing in the direction of a definitive settlement. Had we, as officials, tried to influence Garda operational decisions in that way, it is likely that some tribunal would still be struggling with the allegation that officials had tried to compromise the Garda commissioner's operational independence. We simply outlined to the gardaí what had been said to us and allowed them to factor this information into their own decisions. To their credit, they did this by exercising well-judged restraint on many occasions. It required imaginative leadership to adjust the habits of a lifetime in dealing with the IRA. The leadership of An Garda Síochána was aware from us that there was a realistic chance to bring about peace. While never losing sight of their proper role, or forgetting the grave losses that the force had suffered, the gardaí were as supportive as they could be. In fact, they made a vital, if often unsung, contribution to the peace process.

A similar situation arose in the case of prisoners. There was a view among some—certainly not all—on the British side that the Irish government was 'soft' on republicans. Some of the circumstances surrounding the content, enforcement and judicial interpretations of extradition law probably contributed to this belief and clouded the fact that hundreds of IRA prisoners were held in Irish prisons. The prisons policies adopted here, in the case of republicans, differed to those in the UK. This would have been known in the UK and, very likely, contributed further to the myth of Irish government 'softness'. The fact that IRA inmates insisted on conducting their business with prison governors through the inmate whom they designated 'officer commanding' within the prison, and that they generally presented themselves as an incarcerated army, was not a matter of high priority for us. We were not going to treat as a principle something that could lead to deadly stand-offs and, ultimately, increased support for paramilitary organisations. What mattered was that there was a clear understanding that, once inside the prison walls, the policy of the authorities was that IRA prisoners, like all other prisoners, should remain inside. The presence of armed military personnel on the walls of Portlaoise prison, where most IRA prisoners were held, served as a grim reminder that the government, far from being soft, was determined that this message should be clearly understood.

It had long been the policy of the Irish government that ex-IRA prisoners would not be allowed visits to IRA inmates. However, the case was made to us by Sinn Féin leaders that this rule should be relaxed, because prisoners were an extremely important grouping in terms of advancing the peace process and it would therefore be essential to allow senior republican representatives, who might have served time in the past but were now pro-peace, into the prisons to brief inmates on what was happening politically. The minister for justice has wide discretion in these matters so, with ministerial agreement, we were able to facilitate these visits with little fuss. The case was also made to us, at times, that a particular prisoner should be granted temporary release to attend important peace information meetings on the outside, and this too was facilitated.

Trying to give advice as to how the IRA might or might not react to particular proposals, or what approaches might draw them further along the road towards exclusively peaceful means meant listening carefully to what Sinn Féin representatives were actually saying (or half-saying). It also meant studying carefully the content of IRA statements whenever they emerged. Ministers and civil servants on both sides paid close attention to these statements, which were generally taken as a reasonably accurate indicator as to where the IRA stood in terms of a complete cessation of violence (though it could never be assumed that a statement that seemed positive amounted to a guarantee that there would be no more IRA 'spectaculars' such as the Canary Wharf bombing in 1996, which came within a whisker of putting the whole process indefinitely on ice).

The IRA worded its statements quite carefully and seemed anxious to be able to say at all times that it kept its word even if, to the casual reader, a subsequent IRA action appeared to be in clear contradiction of a recently issued statement. What ministers and officials often searched for, in looking at IRA statements, was evidence of 'wriggle-room'. Suspected wriggle-room language was the subject of a fair share of conversation and speculation: for example, why the IRA said that it planned to put 'arms' beyond use but not 'all arms' beyond use.

It isn't inevitably the case that the infamous wriggle-room, or its half-sister ambiguity, have a malign purpose. If the purpose is to gain the support of a hesitant minority for a statement or a document otherwise widely supported—by leaving doubters with the comfort of seeing a possible exit route or space for a different interpretation—it is one thing. But if it is an attempt to mislead by masking a positive intention to take the exit route, it is an entirely different matter. Ultimately the purpose being served by ambiguity was a matter of judgement and trust. Trust was a commodity that was in fairly short supply for much of the time, and it is not surprising in those circumstances that both governments spent time going carefully through IRA statements.

A level of ambiguity can be necessary at times to draw the widest possible number across a line towards agreement. And a peace agreement that was opposed by a significant number of IRA members would have represented a real—possibly a fatal—challenge to the chance of delivering peace.

There are human realities involved in these processes. I believe, for example, that had the taoiseach and the prime minister decided, in the final hours of the 1998 Good Friday negotiations, to give everybody a badly needed rest period, there was every prospect that people returning refreshed to the talks table would have tried to iron out any gaps or ambiguities that were causing them unease.

That exercise, had it commenced, could well have put paid to the chances of agreement on Good Friday 1998.

Fortunately, the prospect of announcing that a comprehensive agreement had been reached was seen by the two leaders and by others as a prize large enough to generate a level of euphoria that would sweep in its tide any lingering concerns about textual imperfections in the document. An enormous tide of euphoria and goodwill was needed all round to make some of what had been agreed, later in the process, palatable to the great majority of law-abiding people north and south, most notably the decision to grant early release to IRA and loyalist prisoners who had, in some cases, been convicted in the relatively recent past of very serious offences for which they were due to serve long prison terms. The Good Friday Agreement would not have been possible without agreement on those releases and, equally, the releases could only have been contemplated in circumstances in which a major agreement was also being announced.

Returning briefly to the issue of IRA statements and the attention paid to them, I recall that at some meetings with Sinn Féin leaders when the matter of statements was being discussed, I was asked what kind of IRA statement I thought would give both governments assurance that the IRA was committed to exclusively peaceful means. Indeed, on more than one occasion, I found myself sitting down on a Sunday night, after the *Sunday Game* sports programme on RTÉ, trying to draft wordings for IRA statements that would usually be shared in the days that followed with civil service colleagues, on both sides, for further 'sculpting'. I thought it a major fall from grace that I should find myself as secretary general of the Department of Justice, with absolutely no paramilitary credentials, trying to draft IRA statements on a Sunday night—or any night, for that matter.

There was never any prospect that 'P. O'Neill' (the name in which IRA statements were issued) would issue a statement drafted by a non-family member, but the exercise was not, on that account, a totally futile one. It was not entirely a matter of Sinn Féin getting tiresome officials off its back about desired words by giving them pointless homework (though it felt that way at times). What it enabled us to do, over time, was to get words or concepts into the conversations we were having with Sinn Féin, and some of these

178

were probably helpful in terms of inching closer to what we wanted to hear eventually from the IRA.

The topic of arms decommissioning has been covered in many accounts of the peace process, and I do not propose to go into very much detail here. It was inevitable that the subject would feature in the negotiations and very understandable that people who had been victims of IRA and loyalist violence would demand explanations as to why, if those organisations claimed that they were really serious about making peace, they needed to retain large quantities of explosives and arms that couldn't by any stretch of the imagination be described as self-protection weapons. While the topic would have to be addressed, however, many of us felt that it found its way onto the talks table much sooner than was desirable or advisable. There are differences of opinion as to how this came about, which have been the subject of comment by others. An unfortunate effect of its coming on the table in the way and at the time it did was that it gave the IRA—and not only the IRA—a means of stopping and starting progress in the talks and blocking conversations on other matters that needed to be discussed if there was to be a comprehensive agreement.

It was for this reason that the Independent International Commission on Decommissioning (IICD), chaired by General John de Chastelain, was brought into being. The basic idea was to move decommissioning off the main talks table and to empower the IICD to progress the issue away from the limelight by means of direct contact with a representative of the IRA. Moving the subject to a parallel track meant that the risk of its being used to slow or halt negotiations on other issues was greatly reduced.

The train didn't always run smoothly, however, on this parallel track. The IICD reported progress on an ongoing basis to ministers on both sides, in our case the minister for justice, which in practice meant that Ken O'Leary and I regularly met with John de Chastelain, Andy Sens and Tauno Nieminen and some of their support team for briefings. From these meetings it was clear that progress with the IRA was, at times, close to zero. In these situations it fell to both governments in consultation with the IICD and with Sinn Féin representatives to see what could be done to get the process moving more quickly and more smoothly.

A central issue was how the IRA might decommission arms in a way that would remove any suggestion of IRA surrender and at the same time meet the basic requirements of the law. All sorts of ideas were canvassed; some of them, in retrospect, would have involved what can best be described as novel interpretations of the law and very colourful use of the English language.

The very word 'decommissioning' appeared to create immediate difficulties for the IRA because it carried the notion of surrender and the impression that arms would be taken from the IRA and destroyed by others. This is why we came up with the concept of 'putting arms beyond use'. Many of the decommissioning meetings with the IICD, Sinn Féin and our British counterparts took place at Clonard Monastery in Belfast. Those in attendance, apart from Ken and myself, were usually John de Chastelain, Tauno Nieminen and Andy Sens from the IICD, Jonathan Powell and a Northern Ireland Office official on the British side and, for Sinn Féin, Gerry Adams, the late Martin McGuinness and sometimes one or two others. The Sinn Féin team was usually in listening mode and offering to use 'best endeavours' with the IRA to secure progress. Ken and I spent so much time at Clonard during one period that we concluded, when walking one day in the monastery garden, that we must by now have qualified for holy orders and that we should perhaps ask the late and great peace facilitator Father Alex Reid whether he might be able to use his 'best endeavours' to have us both admitted permanently to the monastery.

Those of us who met at Clonard and elsewhere knew in our hearts that while the IRA would probably make some decommissioning gestures for the purpose of showing intent, there was no real likelihood that full decommissioning would take place until it was clear that what had been promised by the governments was being delivered. That said, the constant engagement with Sinn Féin representatives meant that the requirement to deliver on decommissioning remained very much alive. Negotiations don't always produce immediate results, but they buy time and maintain a sense of forward movement: Sinn Féin needed time to bring all its supporters on board, and a sense of forward movement was needed by everybody participating in the process.

I want to conclude this piece with some details of what might be described as the more 'operational' side of our work. In the year 2000 the IRA agreed to allow its arms dumps to be checked and sealed by independent international inspectors. While the move to allow inspections fell short of arms decommissioning, it was nevertheless a welcome development at the time. The agreed inspectors were Mr Martti Ahtisaari, president of Finland and Nobel Peace Prize laureate, and Mr Cyril Ramaphosa of the ANC and now president of South Africa.

One of the first challenges was to get both men into and out of the state without attracting media attention. It was clear that if the media got any hint of what was taking place, the temptation to discover the whereabouts of the inspectors and follow them would be considerable. It was made clear to us also that if the IRA got any sense they were being followed, the whole mission would be aborted. Ken and I sat down to work out exactly what we would do.

One of our first steps was to acquire new mobile phones for Ken and the two inspectors to minimise the risk that conversations between them and with the assigned republican contact might be overheard. How effective this strategy was likely to be I have no idea, but Ken and I understood that the regular purchase of new phones was in accordance with best practice within the criminal fraternity as a means of ensuring that their phone contacts would escape detection—if the use of so-called burners was good enough for them, it was good enough for us!

We then met with the commissioner of An Garda Síochána about some of the logistical arrangements that could be brought into play. I thought it would be helpful if the inspectors were provided with some briefing on the background to the peace process before they arrived (they already had some), and I could think of nobody more suited to this task than Martin Mansergh. Not only is Martin a distinguished historian, he also had years of background work in peace endeavours. Martin and Ken travelled to Paris, with their UK counterparts, to ensure not only that the inspectors had a solid briefing from an Irish government perspective but also that everything ran according to plan.

We felt that it would be too risky to take the two inspectors to any Dublin hotel, and it wouldn't be much better if we took them to a decent guest house, so I decided to seek the assistance of an old friend, the late Monsignor John Greehy, then parish priest at St Joseph's church in Terenure. Monsignor John, born in 1931 and reared in Buttevant, Co. Cork, was an internationally respected biblical scholar. He was described by *The Irish Times* as a 'radical pastor', and I know some who were drawn to Mass in Terenure on Sundays on the prospect—often realised—that he would drift outside the usual sermon boundaries and into matters such as the immorality of policies being pursued by the World Bank, or the shallowness of editorials contained in the Sunday newspapers on sale nearby.

I had enlisted the good offices of the monsignor on a previous occasion to enable a woman prisoner serving a long sentence to attend the christening of her grandchild. So, when it came to the two arms inspectors, I decided that I would again approach him and ask whether the inspectors could be taken from the airport to the presbytery in Terenure, there to await a late-night knock on the door by the republican contact tasked with taking the inspectors to the places of inspection.

Neither of the men who left the presbytery that evening—in republican hands—could conveniently conceal himself behind a whin bush, so Ken and I wondered what fund might be used to compensate some unfortunate sheep farmer for the shock suffered on seeing one or both strange men emerge, possibly at dawn, from a bog-hole in some godforsaken part of Ireland. Fortunately, there was no need to worry; the mission went well and both men were later returned safe and sound to the presbytery, where they were warmly greeted by the monsignor and his housekeeper Maureen, before they headed back to Paris to prepare what was a very welcome and valuable report at the time. The two men paid a couple of subsequent visits, but I had no part in these. Monsignor Greehy is one of many people who quietly made a contribution to the peace process, and that is why I thought it important now to tell this story.

Some journalists, however, may not be pleased to hear what actually happened. The church yard at St Joseph's is bounded on one side by the presbytery and on the other by the Terenure outlet of the Lidl grocery chain. When the two inspectors visited Terenure, the headquarters of the *Sunday World* newspaper stood on what is now the Lidl site. Unfortunately, we couldn't tell the newspaper at the time that a tasty little news item was unfolding within yards of its front door.

Panel 4 Overview

BARBARA JONES

It somehow seems fitting that I'm writing this piece in Bogotá, straight after a landmark meeting about implementing the Colombian Peace Accords between the new Colombian government and the EU. During that crucial meeting, Eamon Gilmore, former tánaiste and minister for foreign affairs, and now the European Union's special envoy to the peace process, set out a clear pathway forward for the next phase of Colombia's process of peace building. Ireland's role in this process has been decisive and we will open a resident embassy here in January 2019 to deepen the array of new civil and political relations that we hold, which are anchored in solidarity and dialogue about peaceful transformation and its challenges.

The event in Bogotà, twenty years after the Good Friday Agreement and almost precisely 33 years after the Anglo-Irish Agreement, stirs reflection and connections with the very significant panel discussion that I was honoured to chair last March in the Royal Irish Academy.

On the one hand, Eamon Gilmore, like Paddy Teahon, Tim O'Connor, Tim Dalton and David Donoghue and the ministers and taoisigh they served, undoubtedly is a key figure of what might be called the 'building the peace process' generation. As last March's discussion suggested, our panel of negotiators were successors to the pioneering Donlon–Lillis civil service leadership, focused on democratic change as the antidote to injustice and political violence.

And diplomacy delivered the Good Friday Agreement, as it had earlier delivered the Anglo-Irish Agreement and the Downing Street Declaration. Irish public officials supported our world-class politicians from all parties, as Ireland advanced brand-new definitions of equality, respect, identity and sovereignty to secure peace and better British–Irish relations. Security policy delivered too, in spades. The panel reminded us of the high levels of engagement we had with the British and Northern Ireland civil service and political elites, while we Europeanised our national question and leveraged, Archimedes-like, our transatlantic relations to transformative effect.

I salute the candour of the panel in outlining the depth and array of relationships required to deliver the agreement: the central leadership of Ahern, Blair, Clinton, Mitchell, Hume; the women's movement in Northern Ireland; churches—a virtual *meitheal* of persuaders for peace. And there was candour about the dilemmas of engagement with belligerents who believed in change through violence, but we recognise the leadership it took to engage in order to stop the killing and to understand their demands. You make peace with the enemy.

The panel gave testimony to historic success. I loved the eloquence, conviction and unwavering passion and recall of detail about the panelists' own roles. I admired and learned how principle, pragmatism, relationships, values and a dogged determination to stop the violence drove the project.

The crisis in Northern Ireland dominated the work of the Department of Foreign Affairs and the Irish civil service. Dealing with that crisis engaged our security, diplomatic and political leaders. The search for peace became the purpose of public service in those decades. It took up valuable time of our leaders and there was a cost for that in terms of policy development and management of other risks. But perhaps this Royal Irish Academy discussion reminds us that this crisis gifted us a framework for a new agreed Ireland, more plural, more tolerant, more respectful, and more connected with our values. National policy as foreign policy.

The event in Dublin, as today's event in Bogotá, reminds me forcefully that many of us who have been honoured to be engaged in the peace process have gained unique insight into the how and the why of peace-building. My work in Belfast, London and now Latin America teaches me that when we find a context to share that experience, people always say that Irish knowledge and understanding (*conocimiento*) is vital for and supportive of their leadership for peace. 'Ireland understands that it takes time.' This suggests to me that the experience of our politicians, civil servants and civic leaders in Ireland, north and south, can be deployed to help others start on the journey to peace and reconciliation that we are on.

Perhaps our civil service knows more than we think about permanent crisis management and crisis avoidance—in relation to both building a comprehensive peace agreement and in defending it, as we currently are in the Brexit context. The Irish case perhaps also demonstrates that continuity of public service expertise and cross-party support for peace and reconciliation in democracies is a vital factor in avoiding stop/start approaches to ending violence.

I think that the peace process in Ireland has gifted our civil service with a narrative about our culture, and resilience in relentless defence of our interests economically and politically. I am so proud to get the opportunity to work in that spirit daily and to pass on the understandings and values of such a wonderful civil service to our future diplomats and public service.

I had the great honour of meeting John Hume when I was a third secretary, and I thought just to end that I would quote some lines from his Nobel Peace Prize address in Oslo. He said:

> The agreement represents an accommodation that diminishes the self-respect of no political tradition, no group, no individual. It allows all of us—in Northern Ireland and throughout the island of Ireland—to now come together and, jointly, to work together in shared endeavour for the good of all. No-one is asked to yield their cherished convictions or beliefs. All of us are asked to respect the views and rights of others as equal of our own and, together, to forge a covenant of shared ideals based on commitment to the rights of all allied to a new generosity of purpose.

SELECTED READING

Barrington, Donal, 1957 'Uniting Ireland', *Studies* 46, 379–402. Available at: https://www.jstor.org/stable/i30098923.

Collins, Jude, 2018 *Martin McGuinness: the man I knew*. Cork. Mercier Press.

Dorr, Noel, 2017 *Sunningdale: the search for peace in Northern Ireland*. Dublin. Royal Irish Academy.

Erlanger, Steve, 1984 'Ulster policy', *Boston Globe*, 18 April.

Fanning, Ronan, 1982 'Playing it cool: the response of the British and Irish government to the crisis in Northern Ireland, 1968–9', *Irish Studies in International Affairs* 1, no. 3, 23–8.

Finlay, Fergus, 1998 *Snakes and ladders*. Dublin. New Island Books.

FitzGerald, Garret, 1991 *All in a life: an autobiography*. Dublin. Gill & Macmillan.

FitzGerald, Garret, 1993 *Northern Ireland and the politics of reconciliation*. Washington, DC. Cambridge University Press.

Fitzpatrick, Maurice, 2017 *John Hume in America: from Derry to DC*. Dublin. Merrion Press.

Hadden, Tom and Boyle, Kevin, 1989 *The Anglo-Irish agreement: commentary, text, and official review*. London. Sweet & Maxwell.

Hume, John 1986 'The strategy of reconciliation', in James Dooge (ed.), *Ireland in the contemporary world*. Dublin. Gill & Macmillan.

Humphreys, Richard, 2018 *Beyond the border: the Good Friday Agreement and Irish unity after Brexit*. Newbridge, Co. Kildare. Merrion Press.

Keenan, Brendan, 1983 'Irish consider three options for unity', *Financial Times,* 22 August.

Kennedy, Michael *et al.* (eds), 2018 *Documents on Irish foreign policy XI*, Document no. 251, 1 January 1960, 322–3. Dublin. Royal Irish Academy.

Keogh, Dermot and Haltzel, Michael (eds), 1993 *Northern Ireland and the politics of reconciliation*. Washington, DC. Cambridge University Press.

Lee, J.J., 1989 *Ireland 1912–1985: politics and society*. Cambridge. Cambridge University Press.

Lillis, Michael and Goodall, David, 2010 'Edging towards peace', *Dublin Review of Books* 107.

Mallie, Eamonn and McKittrick, David, 1996 *The fight for peace: the secret story behind the Irish peace process*. London. Heinemann.

Maryfield Secretariat Witness Seminar, 8 December 2015 'Bunker days', *Dublin Review of Books*. Available at: http://www.drb.ie/essays/bunker-days.

Moriarty, Gerry, 2018 'On the brink of civil war: the two dark weeks that still haunt Northern Ireland', *Irish Times*, 19 March.

McKeever, Martin, 2017 *One man, one God: the peace ministry of Fr Alec Reid CSsR*. Dublin. Redemptorist Communications.

McKittrick, David and McVea, David, 2000 *Making sense of the Troubles*. Belfast. Blackstaff Press.

Moloney, Ed, 2002 *A secret history of the IRA*. London. W.W. Norton.

Nordheimer, Jon, 1983 'Irish leaders seek blueprint for reunion', *New York Times*, 31 May.

O'Connor, Fionnuala, 1993 *In search of a state: Catholics in Northern Ireland*. Belfast. Blackstaff Press.

O'Leary, Brendan and McGarry, John, 2016 *The politics of antagonism: understanding Northern Ireland*. London. Bloomsbury.

O'Leary, Olivia, 1984 'How Charlie swung the Forum', *Magill*, May.

Powell, Jonathan, 'Good Friday Agreement at 20: worth celebrating?' Available at: http://qpol.qub.ac.uk/good-friday-agreement-worth-celebrating/.

Report of the New Ireland Forum, 1984. Available at: http://cain.ulst.ac.uk/issues/politics/nifr.htm#frame.

Reynolds, Albert, 2009 *My autobiography*. Dublin. Transworld Ireland.

Routledge, Paul 1997, *John Hume: a biography*. London. Harper Collins.

Sheridan, Frank, 2016 'The New Ireland Forum', unpublished MPhil thesis, Trinity College Dublin.

Spencer, Graham (ed.), 2015 *The British and peace in Northern Ireland*. Cambridge. Cambridge University Press.

White, Barry, 1984 *John Hume: statesman of the Troubles*. Belfast. Blackstaff Press.

SELECT CHRONOLOGY

Only dates of events mentioned in the volume are given

Year	Date	Event
1965	14 January	Taoiseach Seán Lemass and Northern Ireland Prime Minister Terence O'Neill meet at Stormont: the first meeting between prime ministers of the south and the north since 1922
1966	10 November	Seán Lemass resigns; Jack Lynch becomes taoiseach
1968	24 August	Northern Ireland Civil Rights Association march, Coalisland to Dungannon
	5 October	Civil rights march in Derry results in violence
1969	1 May	Northern Ireland Prime Minister Terence O'Neill resigns; succeeded by James Chichester-Clark
	12–15 August	Rioting in Derry and Belfast; British troops on the streets
	20 September	Jack Lynch Tralee speech
1970	May–June	Arms crisis: Jack Lynch dismisses Cabinet ministers Charles Haughey and Neil Blaney
	18 June	UK general election; Conservative government led by Ted Heath

1971	1 May	Northern Ireland Prime Minister James Chichester-Clark resigns; succeeded by Brian Faulkner
	9–10 August	Introduction of internment in Northern Ireland
	6–7 September	Meeting between taoiseach, British prime minister and British and Irish foreign ministers at Chequers
	27–28 September	Second British–Irish summit at Chequers; Lynch and Heath are joined by Brian Faulkner, prime minister of Northern Ireland
1972	30 January	Bloody Sunday, Derry: thirteen men shot dead by British soldiers
	24 March	Northern Ireland parliament is prorogued and direct rule introduced. William Whitelaw is appointed secretary of state for Northern Ireland
1973	1 January	Ireland and the UK become members of the EEC
	28 February	Irish general election; Fine Gael/Labour coalition government; Liam Cosgrave becomes taoiseach
	20 March	British white paper on constitutional proposals for Northern Ireland is published
	28 June	Northern Ireland Assembly elections
	17 September	Ted Heath meets Liam Cosgrave at Baldonnel aerodrome
	6–9 December	Talks on future government of Northern Ireland at Sunningdale are attended by representatives of Irish and British governments and Northern Ireland Assembly
1974	1 January	Power-sharing executive takes office in Northern Ireland
	28 February	UK general election; Labour government; Harold Wilson becomes prime minister
	14 May	Beginning of Ulster Workers' Council strike
	28 May	Northern Ireland Prime Minister Brian Faulkner resigns; Northern Ireland Executive falls
1977	16 June	Irish general election; Fianna Fáil government; Jack Lynch becomes taoiseach

1977	30 August	Statement by US President Jimmy Carter on Northern Ireland
1978	18 January	Judgment of European Court of Human Rights, Strasbourg, in Ireland v UK case on internment and torture
1979	3 May	UK general election; Conservative government; Margaret Thatcher becomes prime minister
	29 September	Pope John Paul II visits Ireland
	7 December	Jack Lynch resigns; Charles Haughey becomes taoiseach
1980	21 May	First meeting between Charles Haughey and Margaret Thatcher in London
	27 October–18 December	First hunger strike by republican prisoners in Northern Ireland
1981	1 March	Beginning of hunger strike by republican prisoners in the Maze Prison
	5 May	Death of Bobby Sands on hunger strike
	11 June	Irish general election; Fine Gael/Labour coalition government; Garret FitzGerald becomes taoiseach
	3 October	End of hunger strikes. Ten prisoners have died
1982	18 February	Irish general election; Fianna Fáil government; Charles Haughey becomes taoiseach
	May	Falklands war
	24 November	Irish general election; Fine Gael/Labour government; Garret FitzGerald becomes taoiseach
1983	30 May	Formal opening of New Ireland Forum
	9 June	UK general election; Conservative government; Margaret Thatcher remains prime minister
	7 November	First meeting of Anglo-Irish intergovernmental council
1984	2 May	Report of New Ireland Forum is published
	12 October	IRA bomb at Brighton hotel during Conservative party conference; five deaths
	19 November	'Out, out, out' speech by Margaret Thatcher following meeting with Taoiseach Garret FitzGerald

1985	15 November	Hillsborough Agreement
	11 December	First meeting of Anglo-Irish intergovernmental conference
1987	14 February	Irish general election; Fianna Fáil government; Charles Haughey becomes taoiseach
1989	15 June	Irish general election
	12 July	Fianna Fáil/Progressive Democrat coalition government; Charles Haughey remains taoiseach
1990	9 November	Statement in UK parliament by Peter Brooke, secretary of state for Northern Ireland, that Britain has 'no selfish strategic or economic interest in Northern Ireland'
	27 November	John Major succeeds Margaret Thatcher as prime minister
1991	3 July	End of talks sponsored by Peter Brooke, secretary of state for Northern Ireland
1992	6 February	Albert Reynolds succeeds Charles Haughey as taoiseach
	29 April	Opening of multi-party talks in Northern Ireland convened by Patrick Mayhew, secretary of state for Northern Ireland
	10 November	1992 collapse of Brooke–Mayhew talks
1993	12 January	Fianna Fáil/Labour coalition government is formed
	20 November	John Hume/Gerry Adams joint statement
	15 December	The Downing Street Declaration is issued by Albert Reynolds and John Major
1994	31 August	Provisional IRA announcement of 'a complete cessation of hostilities'
	13 October	Combined Loyalist Military Command announces it will 'universally end all operational hostilities'
	15 November	Labour Party resigns from Irish coalition government
	15 December	Coalition government of Fine Gael, Labour and Democratic Left; John Bruton becomes taoiseach

1995	22 February	Irish and British governments publish 'Frameworks for the Future Agreement' document
	28 November	British–Irish governmental strategy to reactivate inter-party talks and examine decommissioning question
1996	6 February	Canary Wharf bombing; end of IRA ceasefire
	30 May	Elections held for Northern Ireland Forum
	10 June	Multi-party talks begin at Stormont
	14 June	First meeting of Northern Ireland Forum
1997	1 May	UK general election; Labour government; Tony Blair becomes prime minister
	6 June	Irish general election; Fianna Fáil/Progressive Democrat coalition, Bertie Ahern becomes taoiseach
	19 July	IRA resumes ceasefire
	9 September	Sinn Féin joins multi-party talks
	15 September	All-party talks begin
	24 September	International panel on decommissioning, headed by General de Chastelain, begins work
1998	20 February	Temporary expulsion of Sinn Féin from talks process because of republican killings
	10 April	Good Friday Agreement is signed
	22 May	Referendums in Ireland and in Northern Ireland endorse the Good Friday Agreement and the deletion of articles 2 and 3 of the Irish constitution
	25 June	Elections to Northern Ireland Assembly
	1 July	First meeting of Northern Ireland Assembly
	8 August	Loyalist Volunteer Force ceasefire
	15 August	Omagh car bomb: 29 people killed
	22 August	Irish National Liberation Army ceasefire
2001	1 October	First report by international Panel on Decommissioning
2002	14 October	Northern Ireland Assembly is suspended
2006	11–13 September	St Andrews Agreement
2007	8 May	First meeting of new Northern Ireland Assembly

Members and Secretariat of the New Ireland Forum

FIANNA FÁIL (MEMBERS AND ALTERNATES)

Charles J. Haughey TD, Brian Lenihan TD, David Andrews TD, Gerry Collins TD, Eileen Lemass TD, Ray MacSharry TD, Rory O'Hanlon TD, Jim Tunney TD, John Wilson TD, David Molony TD, Paudge Brennan TD, Jackie Fahey TD, Jimmy Leonard TD, John O'Leary TD (Secretary: Veronica Guerin).

FINE GAEL (MEMBERS AND ALTERNATES)

Garret FitzGerald TD (Taoiseach), Peter Barry TD (Minister for Foreign Affairs), Myra Barry TD, Senator James Dooge, Paddy Harte TD, John Kelly TD, Enda Kenny TD, Maurice Manning TD, Nora Owen TD, Ivan Yates TD (Secretary: John Fanagan).

LABOUR PARTY (MEMBERS AND ALTERNATES)

Dick Spring TD (Tánaiste and Minister for Energy), Frank Cluskey TD, Senator Stephen McGonagle, Frank Prendergast TD, Mervyn Taylor TD, Eileen Desmond TD, Senator Mary Robinson (Secretary: Diarmaid McGuinness).

SOCIAL DEMOCRATIC AND LABOUR PARTY (MEMBERS AND ALTERNATES)

John Hume MP, MEP, Seamus Mallon, Austin Currie, Joe Hendron, E.K. McGrady, Sean Farren, Frank Feely, Hugh Logue, Paddy O'Donoghue, Paschal O'Hare (Secretary: Denis Haughey).

Tim Dalton served as secretary general of the Department of Justice and Equality, 1993–2004. During that time he was actively engaged in work that supported the search for peace in Northern Ireland, before and after the Good Friday Agreement, with specific focus on justice, security and decommissioning. He is a member of the Commission on the Future of Policing in Ireland, and chair of the Independent Commission for the Location of Victims' Remains.

Mary E. Daly MRIA is professor emerita in modern Irish history at UCD and a member of the Expert Advisory Group on Commemorations. She served as president of the Royal Irish Academy, 2014–17. Her recent publications include *Sixties Ireland: reshaping the economy, state and society, 1957–73* (Cambridge University Press, 2016), and *The Cambridge social history of modern Ireland* (Cambridge University Press, 2017), co-edited with Eugenio F. Biagini.

Catherine Day MRIA is a former secretary general of the European Commission, a post she held for ten years. She is currently chairing the governing body of UCC and the board of trustees of the Chester Beatty Library.

Seán Donlon is a former diplomat (1963–87), executive vice-president of Guinness Peat Aviation (1987–94), special adviser to Taoiseach John Bruton (1994–7), chancellor of the University of Limerick (2002–7) and executive director of the European Bank for Reconstruction and Development (2013–16). He currently chairs the Press Council of Ireland.

David Donoghue worked for many years on the Northern Ireland issue and Anglo-Irish relations in the Department of Foreign Affairs, serving three spells in the department's Anglo-Irish Division (1975–6, 1985–7 and 1991–5). He supported the negotiations on the Anglo-Irish Agreement (1985) and contributed directly to the negotiation of the Downing Street Declaration (1993), the Framework Document (1995), and the Good Friday Agreement (1998). He served as Irish joint-secretary at the Anglo-Irish Secretariat in Belfast from 1995 to 1999 and was posted to the Irish embassy in London from 1988 to 1991, with responsibilities relating mainly to Northern Ireland. He retired from the Irish foreign service in 2017.

Noel Dorr MRIA, a retired Irish diplomat, served as Ireland's permanent representative to the UN and its representative on the Security Council, Irish ambassador in London, and secretary general of the Department of Foreign Affairs. His most recent book is *Sunningdale: the search for peace in Northern Ireland* (Royal Irish Academy, 2017).

Fergus Finlay, former CEO of the Barnardos children's charity and previously adviser to the Irish Labour Party, was senior adviser to Tánaiste and Minister for Foreign Affairs Dick Spring throughout the mid-1990s.

Barbara Jones is Irish ambassador to Mexico; she also represents Ireland in Cuba, El Salvador, Costa Rica, Nicaragua, Venezuela, Colombia and Peru. She has served as consul-general in New York, joint-secretary of the British-Irish Intergovernmental Secretariat in Belfast, special adviser in the Department of the Taoiseach and in the Irish embassy in London, where her role included political relations and the Northern Ireland peace process.

Michael Lillis joined the Department of Foreign Affairs in 1966. He was political counsellor in the Irish embassy in Washington, DC, in 1976–9 and was centrally involved in the negotiation of the 'Carter initiative' on Northern Ireland of August 1977, with President Carter's White House, John Hume, Speaker O'Neill, Senator Edward Kennedy, Senator Patrick Moynihan, Governor Hugh Carey (all in favour) and the State Department and the British government (opposed). In 1981 Lillis was diplomatic adviser to Taoiseach Garret FitzGerald. Between 1983 and 1985 he was one of the Irish negotiators of the 1985 Anglo-Irish Agreement.

Martin Mansergh MRIA is a former diplomat. During the 1980s and 1990s he was special adviser to successive Fianna Fáil taoisigh. He participated in back-channel discussions with the Sinn Féin leadership in 1988, and from 1992 to 1994, and was part of the government negotiating team leading up to the Good Friday Agreement and its implementation.

Dáithí O'Ceallaigh MRIA joined the Department of Foreign Affairs in 1973. He served in Moscow, London (1977–82), the Anglo-Irish Division (1982–5) and the Anglo-Irish Secretariat (late 1985–87), and as consul general, New York (1987–93) and ambassador to Finland (1993–8). He then returned to HQ at Iveagh House (1998–2001, from 2000 as head of the Anglo-Irish Division), before serving as ambassador to the UK (2001–7) and the UN in Geneva (2007–9).

Margaret O'Callaghan is a historian and political analyst at the School of History, Anthropology, Philosophy and Politics at Queen's University, Belfast. She has taught and published widely on the history and politics of Northern Ireland. Some relevant publications are: 'Conor Cruise O'Brien and the Northern Ireland conflict: formulating a revisionist position', *Irish Political Studies* 33 (2) (2018), 221–31; 'Genealogies of partition: history, history-writing and the Troubles in Ireland', *Critical Review of International Social and Political philosophy* 9 (4) (2006), 619–34; 'Old parchment and water: the Boundary Commission of 1925 and the copperfastening of the Irish border', *Bullán: an Irish Studies Review* 4 (2) (2000), 25–42.

Tim O'Connor is a former senior diplomat of the Irish foreign service and a former secretary general to the president of Ireland. He was a member of the Irish government delegation to the talks that led to the Good Friday Agreement in 1998 and was the inaugural southern joint-secretary of the North–South Ministerial Council.

Sean O hUiginn served as a career diplomat in the Irish foreign service between 1968 and his retirement in 2009. In addition to the Northern Ireland-related posts listed in his contribution, he served as Irish ambassador to Saudi Arabia, Denmark, Germany and Italy, and in secondary accreditations attached to these posts.

Olivia O'Leary MRIA is a political columnist for RTÉ Radio 1's *Drivetime* and presents *The poetry programme* on the same channel. She has worked for many years as a current affairs broadcaster for RTÉ, BBC and ITV.

Richard Ryan lectured in American universities from 1970 to 1973, when he joined the Irish Department of Foreign Affairs. During his posting in London (1983–9) he contributed to the achievement of the 1985 Anglo-Irish Agreement and its follow-up. He was ambassador to Korea, Spain, Algeria, Tunisia, the Netherlands, the Organization for the Prohibition of Chemical Weapons (in The Hague), the Czech Republic, Ukraine and, from 1998 to 2005, the United Nations in New York. He represented Ireland on the UN Security Council during 2001–2 and presided over the council following the events of 11 September 2001. He has published several collections of poetry.

Ted Smyth, having joined the Department of Foreign Affairs in 1972, participated in the Irish peace process as the Irish government's press officer in the United States from 1976 to 1982 before joining the Department of the Taoiseach as deputy head of Government Information Services, later becoming a special advisor to Taoiseach Garret FitzGerald. He served on the secretariat of the New Ireland Forum from 1983 to 1984 and became press officer in the Irish embassy in London following the signing of the Anglo-Irish Agreement. Previous diplomatic postings included the Conference on Security and Cooperation in Europe and the Irish embassy in Portugal. In 1988 he took leave of absence from the diplomatic service, subsequently becoming chief administrative officer of the H.J. Heinz company and executive vice president of McGraw Hill Financial.

Paddy Teahon was secretary general of the Department of the Taoiseach, 1993–2000. He played a significant role in the Northern Ireland peace process and social partnership. He is executive director of UCD Energy Institute and adjunct professor at UCD School of Electrical and Electronic Engineering.

INDEX